words of life

The Bible Day by Day

January-April 2022

SALVATION BOOKS

Contents

Abstract

From the Literary Secretary

Power and Praise

REGULAR readers of *Words of Life* will probably have realised that the writing of this book is in a period of transition. Having benefitted from the consistent inspiration of two previous writers – Majors Beverly Ivany and Christine Clement – we are delighted to have three gifted writers contributing to this first edition of 2022. Two are retired officers living in England; the other – our guest writer for Easter – is an officer from Australia.

Major Howard Webber writes: It is a great privilege to contribute to *Words of Life* and to share with you what I sense God is sharing with me. We may not know what God has in store for us in this new year, but we begin our journey together by considering how God is a God of new things. We then explore the first 16 chapters of the Old Testament book of 1 Samuel. Though mankind may disappoint and frustrate God, he never gives up on us and encourages us to never give up on him.

In the Acts of the Apostles we look at five unalike disciples, focusing particularly on a very different Peter than the one we knew in the Gospels, and then – familiar as they may be – there is always something new to discover as we watch Jesus performing miracles. Beautiful Bible blessings and benedictions conclude our journey, and I pray that you will each continue to experience God's blessings on a daily basis.

Lieut-Colonel Margaret Wickings writes: The subject for most weekend reflections is 'Songs in the Night: Singing in Adversity'. The Bible contains many of them. Not all of them look like songs, of course; not all have poetic structure. Most do not tell us which tunes to use – and when they do (in some psalms, for instance), we no longer have those tunes. Even so, we can sense the hearts and spirits of the writers behind the words used; their joy or pain, anxiety or bewilderment, courage or hope. We find ourselves identifying with them as they stir our own hearts. That is what songs do: they take us beyond mere words, to a deeper level – a soul-level. Through them our spirits are lifted; we can find new hope and courage; a new desire to draw closer to Jesus – and sometimes new challenge too. God uses songs to reach past our rational thoughts and touch our hearts. Allow him to do that for you, as you read.

As you progress through these readings, be blessed while you allow our writers' words to bring new insights to familiar Bible passages and, in turn, I pray that you will be a blessing to others.

Paul Mortlock
International Headquarters, London, UK

New every morning

...for his compassions never fail. They are new every morning (vv 22-23)

WE have a new year with new things ahead, so you may well ask: 'Why start it with a passage from Lamentations?'

The Jews in exile in Babylon had gone through an horrendous experience. They had suffered terribly and lost so much that was dear to them. They knew life would never be the same again. They also knew it was something that God planned long ago, something he had held back from doing for centuries, something he promised he would do if the nation did not repent and turn from their sin.

1:12

2:17

Leviticus 26:17

Yet, despite believing it was God in his wrath who had afflicted them, and it was what the nation deserved, they still believed their God to be a God of love and that his compassions, his blessings, never fail and were new every morning.

v 42

You may have had a terrible 2021 and wondered why God allowed you to experience the things you did. It's highly unlikely to have been his punishment for sin. When Jesus healed the man born blind, his disciples assumed his blindness was God's punishment for his or his parents' sins, but Jesus repudiated that idea. It's also highly unlikely that you will get an answer as to the why, any more than righteous Job did following what he went through.

John 9:1-3

While you may be hoping 2022 will be a better year, the road ahead might seem dark indeed. We, like the writer of Lamentations, need to call to mind the facts (though they might conflict with how we feel or how things might appear) that God loves us with a great love, a great unfailing love. Isn't it amazing that they still saw God that way?

vv 22, 32

Amid the darkest of days God's compassions will not fail, they are new every morning. He reveals his love for us in a new way every day – if only we have eyes to see.

PRAYER

Lord, though my tears may be many, make me aware of your unfailing love each day.

A new command

'A new command I give you: love one another' (v 34)

v 27

FOLLOWING the Last Supper, Judas left the company of the others, having been told by Jesus to quickly do what he was about to do. Jesus then gave final instructions to his 11 remaining disciples. He spoke to them as a parent would speak to their offspring, referring to them as, 'My children.' Although he also spoke of God as being his Father and he being his Son, like the song says:

> Fatherlike he tends and spares us;
> Well our feeble frame he knows,
> In his hands he gently bears us,
> Rescues us from all our foes.   (Henry Francis Lyte)

SASB 55 v 3

Isaiah 9:6, the popular verse read during Advent, is considered by Christians to refer to Jesus and describes him thus:

> Wonderful Counsellor, Mighty God,
> Everlasting Father, Prince of Peace.

Parents long for their children to live in harmony. Nothing breaks a parent's heart more than offspring who do not love each other. Jesus could not have emphasised more clearly the importance he put on his disciples loving one another.

First, he placed this new command right at the beginning of what he had to say. Secondly, it wasn't a request, a hope, a pipe dream. It was a command! Thirdly, in just those two verses he states it *three* times.

vv 34-35

If the disciples had any questions regarding the quality of the love they were to have for each other, Jesus made it clear: '*As I have loved you*, so you *must* love one another.' Powerful words! That love for each other would be how the world would recognise them as Christ's disciples, he said.

1 John 4:7-21

Tertullian, a Roman theologian AD 160-225, spoke of how impressed pagan observers were by that love: 'See how these Christians love one another,' they were heard to say.

I wonder, is that the hallmark of our church? Of me – and you?

PRAYER
Father, fill me with that love for others which you have for me.

A new creation

Therefore, if anyone is in Christ, that person is a new creation: the old has gone, the new is here! (v 17)

I WONDER if a caterpillar ever imagines it might one day be a beautiful butterfly, flying high from flower to flower, as opposed to having to clamber up plants to find leaves to eat? The two creatures are so different they would hardly seem related to one another.

For that caterpillar to become a beautiful butterfly it needs to be 'born again'. So, too, with me and you. God doesn't wish us to be just improved versions of what we once were. He wants us to be new people, no longer thinking and viewing life how once we did.

John 3:1-12

v 16

When born again, our whole perspective and reason for living changes. Life is no longer about what we desire or think best, but what Jesus would have us be and do. The old self has to die and be replaced by Christ living his life in and through us. That change is something anyone who knows us will notice.

v 15

Galatians 2:20

In his quest for self-knowledge, Richard Slater (known as the 'Father of Salvation Army Music') attended a number of places of worship. His curiosity at what he read in the newspapers about The Salvation Army led him to attend a meeting in Hampstead in July 1882.

There, a young uneducated servant-girl got up and blurted out, 'My missus says she believes I am saved, because I sweep beneath the mats now, and I didn't before.' Slater recorded how her words impressed him far more 'than all the sermons I had ever heard'. That humble servant-girl, once a caterpillar, had become one of God's beautiful butterflies.

Born again; a new creation; we are but babes in Christ. God still has much to do to bring us to maturity in him, but already we are not who once we were. Hallelujah!

PRAYER

Finish then thy new creation, pure and spotless let us be;
Let us see thy great salvation, perfectly restored in thee.
Changed from glory into glory, till in Heaven we take
   our place,
Till we cast our crowns before thee, lost in wonder,
   love and praise.   (Charles Wesley)

SASB 262 v 3

Newborn babies

Like newborn babies, crave pure spiritual milk, so that by it you may grow up in your salvation (v 2)

DO those of you who are parents remember your sleep at night being punctuated by the cry of your newborn baby? You knew the cause was most likely to be one of three things: the little one needed their nappy changing, had wind that was causing pain, or was hungry. In most cases in those early days it was the latter. That cry, often every four hours, couldn't be ignored and only got louder the longer you delayed responding. Nothing less than the milk they craved would satisfy them.

As babies grow, slowly they are weaned from depending on milk alone to eating solid food. The baby/toddler will still depend on someone else feeding them. It will take some time before they are able to feed themselves.

So too, spiritually. Newborn babes in Christ are rarely capable of feeding themselves; they need help, support, encouragement and teaching from others. But it is important they learn to do so and that they do not remain infants but mature in their faith.

None of us would have grown to adulthood had our only diet been milk. The writer to the Hebrews was concerned about the equivalent issue spiritually. His readers should have matured to become teachers, but they still needed someone to teach them elementary truths of God's Word all over again. 'You need milk not solid food!' he says, making the point that anyone on milk is still an infant.

5:12-13
1 Corinthians
3:1-3

They may well have needed milk but whether they had any real desire to be fed milk is questionable. Had they craved and digested milk, they would surely have been on solid food by now and feeding – that is, teaching – others.

How hungry are we for God and the things of God, I wonder. It's the craving to be fed that Peter emphasises in today's Scripture passage. The psalmist had that craving as well: 'As the deer pants for streams of water, so my soul pants for you, my God.'

Psalm 42:1

PRAYER

Father, give me a real hunger after you, a craving like that of a hungry, thirsty newborn baby.

The new covenant

By calling this covenant 'new', he has made the first one obsolete; and what is obsolete and outdated will soon disappear (v 13)

THE Greek word that the Bible translates as 'a covenant' is *diathēkē*, which actually means a will or testament. A covenant can be between two equal parties with conditions set and agreed among them, but with a last will and testament, the one writing the will – the testator – decides any conditions. The beneficiaries have no say: on the death of the testator, they either accept or reject what the testator decided.

When God gave Moses his laws for the nation, he made a covenant promising his protection and blessing, subject to them obeying him and keeping his laws. When Moses then presented God's covenant to the people, they responded, 'Everything the LORD has said we will do.' Again, while confirming and sealing their commitment with blood, they declared, 'We will do everything the LORD has said; we will obey.' Exodus 20:1–23:19 / 23:20 33 / 23:22 / 24:3 / 24:7

But the covenant was an external legalistic thing, governed by fear – the fear of the consequences of breaking God's law. By the time of Jesus, that fear had resulted in every aspect of life being examined in minute detail and a rule made as to whether or not it contravened God's law. Ordinary people could not possibly know, memorise and keep it all, and the religious professionals who did, self-righteously looked down on ordinary people with contempt.

Although it was out of his mercy that God gave that old covenant, the nation was incapable of fulfilling its requirements. Consequently, Jeremiah, centuries before Jesus came, saw that the day would come when it would be replaced by a new covenant that would not be with the nation but individuals. It would not be external but, as verse 10 of today's Scripture says, written in the heart; not dependent on effort or achievement but faith. 31:31-34

Obedience would not be out of fear but out of love for the wonderful gift of God – Jesus.

PRAYER
Father, thank you for creating a new covenant that does not depend on my merit, but the merit of he who perfectly fulfilled your will, yet suffered the punishment our sins deserved, removing all fear of condemnation from us.

11

A new song

He put a new song in my mouth, a hymn of praise to our God (v 3)

DO you ever have really dark periods of gloom, when you have no sense of God's presence? It seems the Lord has turned away from you and Satan whispers in your ear that God is displeased with you and has abandoned you!

David, the psalmist, was distressed, in a pit – a 'slimy pit'. It is impossible to get out of a pit with slimy sides unless someone reaches down and hauls us out, and David knew the only one who could haul him out of the quagmire of his depression was God himself.

David speaks of how he waited *patiently*. Help obviously did not come quickly. It seemed as though God had turned away and not heard David's cry. Do you ever feel like that? Yet, despite his despondency, David remained steadfast in believing, hoping and praying that God would rescue him. This was the strong belief of Isaiah too: 'All of you that honor the LORD and obey the words of his servant, the path you walk may be dark indeed, but trust in the LORD, rely on your God.'

50:10 *GNB*

Eventually God lifted David out of the mud and mire – surely a description of his spiritual melancholy and the discouraging lies Satan always seeks to fill our minds with? Set 'on a rock', it was as if he had been transformed into a new world that required a new expression of praise and gratitude. The old songs were just not good enough.

v 17

We know from the rest of the psalm that David's problems had not gone away; he still needed God to help him and deliver him from them, but inwardly God had changed him and verse 3 says those around him would see how different David was.

Matthew 28:20

Jesus knew the agony of the garden and the cross, and a sense that God had abandoned him. His slimy pit was death. He knows how we feel like no other. So, be assured, he will never leave you!

PRAYER

Lord Jesus, when darkness obscures your smiling face, keep me steadfast in believing, hoping and praying that you will lift me out of this deep dark pit I am in.

New wine

Others mocking said, These men are full of new wine (v 13 *KJV*)

INDEED, those first believers – somewhere around 120 of them – were full of new wine, but not as those who mocked them supposed. They were not drunk, filled with alcohol, but filled with the Holy Spirit.

1:15
2:15

Up until then the Holy Spirit had only been given to particular people, at particular times, for particular purposes – people like Bezalel, Gideon, Samson and Isaiah. What God had promised nearly 400 years earlier, through the prophet Joel, was now being poured out on all those believers, young and old, male and female, of any social standing.

Exodus 31:2-5,
Judges 6:34,
Isaiah 61:1-3,
Judges 15:14

Acts 2:17-21

It was a new experience for them all. Although the Holy Spirit had been at work in their lives – as when Peter's eyes were opened to the fact that Jesus was 'the Messiah, the Son of the Living God' – they had never had the Holy Spirit poured upon them, never been filled with him. Well aware of their previous failings and their limitations, they knew they needed God's promised gift if they were to fulfil God's will for them – and the Holy Spirit brought them 'power from on high', as Jesus promised.

Matthew 16:16

Luke 24:49;
Acts 1:4, 8

A.W. Tozer once wrote, 'If the Holy Spirit was withdrawn from the Church today, 95 per cent of what we do would go on and no one would know the difference. If the Holy Spirit had been withdrawn from the New Testament church, 95 per cent of what they did would stop, and everybody would know the difference.'[1]

God poured out the Holy Spirit on a people who were hungry to have what God wanted to give them in response to their persistent prayers. Like those first believers, without the Holy Spirit filling us we cannot be or do what God would have us be or do. The Spirit's infilling is essential.

Luke 11:9-13

Acts 19:1-7

Is ours a Spirit-filled life? How hungry are we to have the gift God has promised us?

PRAYER
Father, give me a desire that will persist in prayer until I have the gift you promised.

Singing in the night ... when our world turns upside-down

'Praise be to the LORD, the God of Israel, because he has come to his people and redeemed them' (v 68)

IN our weekend readings we will reflect on songs arising out of difficult and challenging situations. And before Christmas becomes a distant memory, we begin with Zechariah today and Mary tomorrow.

Zechariah and his wife Elizabeth had been faithful to God for so many years. Their hearts were right with him; their trust in him strong. And yet, when faced with a challenge so close to his heart, Zechariah's faith failed.

To be a father was his dearest wish, the fulfilment of his manhood as a Jew. It had been denied. The hurt was so deep that when an angel told him it was to happen after all, although Elizabeth had passed far beyond the natural physical possibility, he did not dare to believe in case he was disappointed yet again. Poor Zechariah.

Worse still, he was told that because of his doubts he would be unable to speak until the promise came true. This added insult to injury for him. Why should his natural hesitancy to believe be punished in this way? Imagine the thoughts passing through his mind, then and for the next nine months. He certainly had time to reflect and consider!

And then it happened. The angel's words came true; John [the Baptist] was born. In faithfulness to the angel's message – and despite months of verbal isolation – Zechariah was able to confirm the name given by the angel for his son. It seems he had come to terms with the promise at last.

His song? One of praise and faith (see v 68). God had kept his promise; God *always* keeps his promise. Was Zechariah also experiencing, in that moment, God's loving forgiveness for his doubts? Perhaps.

Sometimes we are asked simply to hold on in faith, even when everything seems to be against us; hanging on by our fingernails perhaps. Zechariah found that God was faithful. God still is – and in the 'hanging on' times he holds us. Let's spend some moments in prayer now, thanking God for his faithfulness through the challenging times. You may find it helpful to write your prayer. You will be surprised by the assurance God gives.

... when our world turns upside-down – Mary

'I am the LORD's servant ... May your word to me be fulfilled' (v 38)

THE coronavirus pandemic has shaken us to the core. Our physical, emotional, mental and spiritual health have all been challenged at depth. What has helped you most, kept you on a reasonably even keel, carried you through?

Mary's song is her response to a frightening situation. She was engaged to Joseph and so probably just a teenager, according to Jewish marriage customs. Her knowledge and understanding of the world, of God and of faith would have been limited to Nazareth, her family and the local synagogue.

In innocence, she accepted the words of the angel – and then was plunged into the questions and accusations of small-town Nazareth; a bewildering experience for anyone, let alone a naïve girl. So she turned to a trusted much older cousin who, amazingly, was passing through a very similar experience.

Mary left Nazareth to spend three months with Elizabeth, presumably to adjust mind, heart and spirit to the practical implications of her situation – and just to escape for a while. Out of those months came Mary's song: 'My soul glorifies the Lord and my spirit rejoices in God my Saviour.' What an amazing response!

As she continues, emphasising the huge honour and blessing of her pregnancy, her spirits rise. She says nothing of her difficulties; she would surely have shared those in depth with cousin Elizabeth – who wouldn't? – and have benefitted from Elizabeth's long experience of the ways of God.

Having shared, Mary was able to look beyond, to focus on God and affirm her own simple trust in him. There is always a place to 'spill the beans' – God provides friends and counsellors to help us in that – but having done so, we look up and allow God to encourage us directly and help us to keep going.

How did you react to the COVID-19 pandemic? How are you responding to it even now? Take time to talk with God about it today. Let him lift your spirits, remind you of his constant love for you, and help you to be strong again. And having done so, perhaps you will sing Mary's song also?

No one understands

'Hannah, why are you weeping? Why don't you eat? Why are you downhearted? Don't I mean more to you than ten sons?' (v 8)

ELKANAH loved his wife, Hannah, deeply. He endeavoured to express his sympathy for her not being able to have children, and to make her feel special. Every year he took his family with him to Shiloh, the nation's worship centre at that time, where he would make his sacrifice to God and then give each of his family a portion of the meat. But to Hannah he gave a double portion as an expression of the love he had for her. Yet hers was not a life of domestic bliss.

Matthew 19:4-5
Genesis 16:1-6,
29:30-31

Unfortunately Elkanah had two wives – something not originally ordained by God, and the cause of trouble for both Abram and Jacob. Elkanah's other wife, Peninnah, had provided him with children, which obviously was a cause of distress to Hannah.

v 6

Yet it must have seemed unfair to Peninnah that she was the one who had provided her husband with children and yet her 'rival' (for they were now rivals for his affection) was the one who received special treatment. Favouritism and jealousy are frequently the cause of family disharmony. Jealous of Hannah, Peninnah made Hannah's stay at Shiloh unbearable. She taunted her regarding her inability to conceive. Reduced to tears, Hannah was unable to eat.

Was Elkanah unaware of what was going on? Was he too busy about his religious duties to notice? Is it possible a person can be so preoccupied in church activity and duties today that they are unaware of needs in their family?

Elkanah loved Hannah dearly, but it seems he had little idea of how she felt. He just couldn't understand why his love for her was not enough. Poor Hannah. Lyrics from a John Gowans song seem so apt:

SASB 10 v 1

> Do you sometimes feel that no one truly knows you,
> And that no one understands or really cares?

Yet, though she felt God himself 'had closed her womb', Hannah never closed her heart to God.

PRAYER
When alone, feeling that no one cares or understands, help me to hold on to you, Lord.

A costly vow

'LORD **Almighty, if you will only look on your servant's misery and remember me, and not forget your servant but give her a son, then I will give him to the LORD for all the days of his life' (v 11)**

WHAT an amazing promise Hannah made in her anguish and bitter tears! Have you ever come before God in such a state? Hannah's promise is our 'key' text for today, and verse 12 shows Hannah persisting with her petitions – something Jesus taught you and me to do. God wants to know just how much we desire what we ask for. 'Pray without ceasing,' says Paul. But our prayers must be in accord with God's desires, which might mean waiting so that his answer will fit in with some wider plan he has.

Luke 11:5-8
1 Thessalonians 5:17 KJV

George Muller, a wonderful Victorian evangelist and great man of prayer, once said, 'When I am once persuaded that a thing is right and for the glory of God, I go on praying for it until the answer comes. The great fault of the children of God is, they do not continue in prayer ... they do not persevere.'

I am sure Hannah had been praying for a son for years, but on that day in Shiloh, in her desperation, she found the key to God opening the door to answering her pleas. She no longer focused on just having her personal longings fulfilled or her shame removed; she focused on God. He had wonderful plans for the child he wanted to give to her, but needed Hannah to realise her need to give that child back to him.

Sometimes God's answer to our prayer is in the wings awaiting entry onto the stage of our lives. But with all the prayers we have prayed, he has yet to hear the one we need to pray – focused on God and what he desires. William Inge described prayer as 'the elevation of the mind (or soul) to God' and quoted George Meredith: 'He who rises from his knees a better man, his prayer has been granted.'

But it is one thing to make a costly vow and quite another to keep it when circumstances change.

PRAYER
> Have I ceased from walking close beside thee?
> Have I grieved thee with an ill-kept vow?
> In my heart of hearts have I denied thee?
> Speak, dear Lord, O speak and tell me now.

        (Will J. Brand)   *SASB* 634 v 2

Appearances can be deceptive

... Eli thought she was drunk and said to her, 'How long are you going to stay drunk? Put away your wine' (vv 13-14)

WE are all prone to do it, to judge according to appearances rather than facts. Chatting with a resident of a hostel for the homeless, he shared with me how he once had a good job, a beautiful home, and a lovely wife and family. He looked on the hostel residents he saw around town as lazy good-for-nothings, wondering why they didn't get themselves jobs instead of depending on state benefits paid from the taxes of hard-working people like himself.

All that changed when his wife left him for another man and took the children with her. He had a breakdown, lost his job, then his home, and landed up sleeping on the streets. Given a place in that same local hostel, he became one of the men for whom previously he had such contempt. The men he then got to know and the stories many shared changed his whole outlook.

Because of Hannah's unusual behaviour, Eli the priest made the assumption that she was drunk, and was quite severe in his condemnation of her. It hurts to be misjudged, condemned.

vv 15-16 Hannah certainly felt it! Eli thought evil of Hannah, being drunk in the Lord's house. It is terrible to think people guilty of unproven bad things.

When we are falsely judged or accused we need to be very careful how we respond. Naturally, we will be upset, perhaps angry, with a desire to fight fire with fire; to accuse the accuser of faults *they* possess. Satan loves us to respond by justifying ourselves in that way. But dear Hannah didn't. She respectfully shared the facts. She didn't allow the hurt she felt to control her response. Neither must we.

On hearing what she had to say, Eli saw his error and blessed her and encouraged her. It would seem the Holy Spirit brought her peace and an assurance of answered prayer at that moment, for she departed and ate something – and 'was no longer downcast'.

PRAYER
Jesus, help me not to judge others and to forgive those who hurtfully misjudge me.

Answered prayer

So in the course of time Hannah became pregnant and gave birth to a son (v 20)

A POSTER outside a church stated, 'A family that prays together stays together,' emphasising the importance of family worship. With our busy lives, where there seems never enough time for everything, family worship and the sharing together of the things of God can so easily be neglected – or left to fit in when everything else has been done.

Despite the problems in Elkanah's family life, worship together was a priority. Although they had a busy day ahead of them, Elkanah and his family were up early to worship God before beginning their journey home to Ramah. And it would seem Hannah already had an assurance of answered prayer and an end to her misery, well before she actually became pregnant. God sometimes reassures us that he has heard and answered prayer ahead of any solid evidence.

vv 18, 20

James Hudson Taylor, who would become a renowned missionary in China, was sceptical about Christianity as a young man because of the inconsistencies he and his pals observed in Christians. Concerned, his mother and sister, Amelia, were both praying for his salvation. One day he wandered into his father's library and picked up a gospel tract with the intention of only reading the introductory story. But he continued with the message that followed, which resulted in him surrendering his life to Christ.

Little did he know that 70 or 80 miles away his mother, staying with friends, had felt prompted to pray for him. She went to her room resolved not to leave until convinced her prayer was answered. She prayed for hours before assurance came. When she returned a fortnight later, James discovered his mother's certainty of his salvation had been given at the precise time he had received it.

Following Samuel's birth, Elkanah agreed Hannah need not go with the family to Shiloh. Perhaps she felt it right to remain at home with little Samuel, knowing she would be without him soon enough.

PRAYER

Father, draw me so close to you that I too will sense your assurance that my prayer has been answered, though visible evidence may be absent. Replace my heartache with your peace.

Giving God our dearest and best

After he was weaned, she took the boy with her, young as he was ... and brought him to the house of the Lord at Shiloh (v 24)

'GOOD night, good night! Parting is such sweet sorrow, that I shall say good night till it shall be morrow,' so says Shakespeare's Juliet to Romeo. This oxymoron (the apparent contradiction between parting being sweet *and* sorrowful) was surely the experience of Hannah. She loved her little boy. Samuel was the son she hoped, dreamed and prayed for over many years, and she had nurtured him in the things of God. God's Word tells us: 'Start children off on the way they should go, and even when they are old they will not turn from it.'

Proverbs 22:6; Deuteronomy 6:7

Samuel was about three years old when Hannah took him to the house of the Lord. It had been at least four years since she last visited Shiloh, so Eli may not have immediately recognised Hannah. She reminded the priest of the promise she made to God and now desired to fulfil it.

I am deeply moved by a picture in my mind's eye of that little toddler arriving at Shiloh, having been told by his mummy what was going to happen. While Mum was talking with Eli, did Samuel toddle off on his own and spontaneously kneel in worship in that place?

v 28

Hannah then prayed a prayer of thanksgiving to God for what he had done for her, before quickly expanding her prayer to one of praise as to who God is – holy, incomparable, the sovereign Lord of everything. As Chris Tomlin's song proclaims:

How great is our God, sing with me,
How great is our God, and all will see
How great, how great is our God.[2]

SASB 64 refrain

So often our prayers are more about God's gifts rather than the Giver.

I wonder how Hannah felt returning home childless? Surely it wasn't without tears? Yet, in Hannah willingly giving her son to God we see something of the heart of God, who later willingly gave his only Son for us.

PRAYER
Lord, deepen my love, my trust and my willingness to give you what might cost me dearly, should you desire it.

Singing in the night ... when we are treated unfairly (1)

About midnight Paul and Silas were praying and singing hymns to God, and the other prisoners were listening to them (v 25)

WHAT a day! Paul and Silas were in Philippi because the Holy Spirit had sent them there (see vv 6-12). Through their ministry Lydia, a well-respected merchant, found Jesus. Her household then followed her example. Lydia was already 'a worshipper of God' (v 14) – a Gentile who followed Jewish ways of worship. Now she had taken the next step.

All was going well for Paul and Silas – and then this trouble over a demon-possessed slave girl!

Did Paul finally lose his temper – perhaps because of the girl's persistent shouts? Imagine the scene: wouldn't you also have felt frustrated by her interruptions? Perhaps Paul was concerned that her shouts diminished the gospel message and distracted others from responding to Jesus in faith. Or maybe he just wanted her to be free.

Whatever the reason, for Paul and Silas the result was catastrophic. The girl's furious owners, motivated both by anger at lost earnings and by prejudice against Jews in general, accused them beyond truth. To quell the growing riot, the authorities beat Paul and Silas and imprisoned them.

And then Paul and Silas sang praises to God in the middle of the night, waking the other prisoners in the process! Were they using praise in protest; an outlet for their anger like the taunts exchanged by opposing football fans? Was it a cynical snub towards the authorities for the treatment they had been given? No, God would be dishonoured and saddened by such misuse of his name.

Although we are not told the words they used, verse 25 implies that their praises and prayers focused on God's faithful presence with them in their situation; their trust in his unfailing love. He would never leave them.

What do you do when *you* are unfairly treated? Do you respond with anger, slander, cynicism? Or do you remind yourself – and those around you – of God's faithfulness despite all? It is quite a challenge but we are not alone. The Holy Spirit has promised to stand with us at such times and remind of all he has taught us (see John 14:15-17, 26-27).

Take time now to talk with God about this and seek his Spirit's help, ready for when challenging times might come.

... when we are treated unfairly (2)

Suddenly there was such a violent earthquake that the foundations of the prison were shaken. At once all the prison doors flew open, and everybody's chains came loose (v 26)

WHAT drama! Take a moment to imagine the earthquake and the release of all the prisoners' chains. No wonder the jailer reacted as he did. He had been tasked with guarding Paul and Silas carefully (vv 23-24). He knew that his own life was at risk if he failed. Interestingly, he did not check to see if any prisoners were still there; he assumed they had fled at the first opportunity.

Paul took charge of the situation. How did he know that no prisoners had escaped? Surely they would instantly rush for the open door? Oh, to have been a fly on the wall of that prison!

When the jailer realised that none of his prisoners had escaped, he was filled with awe concerning Paul and Silas, becoming convinced that the God of whom Paul preached must be greater than the gods which he and his people worshipped. There, in the prison, Paul was privileged to lead him into faith in Jesus; another Gentile now accepting the gospel.

In tending their wounds and taking Paul and Silas to his own house for a meal, the jailer took a huge risk. What if the authorities found out? But such was his joy in his new-found faith that he was prepared to take that risk.

The next day, the authorities sent word to release Paul and Silas. Presumably they had sorted out the cause of the riot and concluded that these two prisoners were innocent after all! But Paul would not go quietly. He knew that the slave girl's owners could still cause ongoing trouble for the new converts, so he used his Roman citizenship to establish respect for the believers within the town. Beating and imprisoning Roman citizens without trial was a serious offence. No one would want to challenge a group whose leader was a Roman citizen.

Paul and Silas sang in the night, after being treated unfairly. As a result, the jailer and his household found Jesus – perhaps some of the prisoners did also – and all the converts in Philippi were protected from further harassment.

It is amazing what singing in faith can do! Why not try it today?

God is nobody's debtor

And the LORD was gracious to Hannah; she gave birth to three sons and two daughters (v 21)

ALWAYS, within the body of God's people, there are those who live for themselves rather than God. Some give all the signs of being sincere, pious and devout, as did the Pharisees whose hypocrisy Jesus exposed. Others, such as Eli's sons, are blatant in their godless ways, caring little about what others think of them.

Luke 11:37-52

Eli's two sons, Hophni and Phinehas, were priests at Shiloh yet scoundrels with no regard for the Lord, and it was common knowledge among the people. What amazing trust, therefore, did Hannah show in God! If Eli was incapable of bringing up godly sons, how could her son's godliness be guaranteed? And what would be the influence of Eli's sons on her little boy as he grew up? But Hannah had not seen herself as giving Samuel to Eli or the house of the Lord, but rather to God himself, trusting him to take care of her little boy.

1:3; 2:12
v 24

1:28

It must have been upsetting and discouraging for worshippers to see their offerings to God treated with contempt by the priests, yet it didn't stop people like Elkanah making their annual pilgrimage to Shiloh.

Are there things in your fellowship that discourage you? Things you feel are wrong, perhaps not dealt with. Have you ever felt like giving up? Paul surely knew something of that when he wrote, 'Let us not give up the habit of meeting together, as some are doing.'

Hebrews 10:25
GNB

When Hannah gave her only son to God there was no evidence that she would ever have another child. But the truth that Hannah discovered, when God blessed her with five more children, is that no one is ever the poorer for giving God the best – whatever the cost or sacrifice. In fact, they will be the richer.

Mark 10:28-30;
Malachi 3:10

Another of Hannah's riches was to see her boy 'grow in stature and favour with the LORD and with people'.

PRAYER
Father God, keep me faithful amid disappointments and discouragements, willing to sacrifice all I love and value, knowing I will never be the poorer for it.

Weakness and wickedness

"'I will raise up for myself a faithful priest, who will do according to what is in my heart and mind. I will firmly establish his priestly house, and they will minister before my anointed one always'" (v 35)

IT wasn't that Eli was evil, it was that he was weak and unwilling to put an end to his sons' abuse of their privileged positions as priests in the house of the Lord. For he knew all that was going on.

v 22

Some attribute Edmund Burke, an Irish statesman and philosopher, with the saying, 'The only thing necessary for the triumph of evil is that good men do nothing.' Sometimes refusal to 'do nothing' can be costly. Satan will gather all the forces at his disposal to oppose the courageous man or woman of God willing to stand up and be counted, as he did in the case of William Wilberforce in his lifelong battle against slavery. The stance that the pastor, theologian Dietrich Bonhoeffer took against Hitler and Nazism cost him his life. If we look the other way or shut our eyes, we cannot claim ignorance – and if we do nothing, we cannot claim innocence.

Proverbs 24:10-12

Despite the wickedness that prevailed in God's house, there were godly people in Israel who God could call upon to do his bidding, and he sent such a person to Eli to spell out exactly how he viewed both him and his sons. From what the man said it seems that Eli benefitted from his sons' sin, eating the choice parts of the meat sacrifice that should have been burnt off as offerings to God.

The man then told Eli what was in store for his family as a result of his sons' wickedness and his complicity in honouring them more than honouring God. God would have honoured them had they honoured him – a promise as valid to you and me today as it was back then to them.

Hebrews 7:24-27
v 35

And though he might not have realised it, the man then foretold the coming of our faithful high priest, Jesus, who did and does what is 'in the heart and mind' of God. How privileged we are to be part of God's holy, royal priesthood, ministering before him.

1 Peter 2:5, 9

PRAYER

Lord Jesus, in all we do and say may we honour you today.

Knowing God

Now Samuel did not yet know the Lᴏʀᴅ (v 7)

THE spiritual life of the nation had declined with corruption at the very centre of its religious life: 'the word of the Lᴏʀᴅ was rare; there were not many visions'. It was a similar spiritual situation as existed prior to the coming of Jesus. There had been no prophetic messages from God since the days of Haggai, Zechariah and Malachi – more than 400 years.

But God still hadn't given up on Israel. He may hide his face in response to our preoccupation with other things and our failure to keep him uppermost in our lives, as he did with them; but as Paul told the Athenians: 'he is not far from any one of us'. God longs that we 'would seek him and perhaps reach out for him and find him'. *see Deuteronomy 31:18 / Acts 17:27*

According to Josephus, the Jewish historian, Samuel was now 12 years old. Sleeping close to the ark of God and within calling distance of Eli, now barely able to see, Samuel was awoken to the sound of his name being called. His immediate reaction was to *run* to Eli, such was his concern for the old man who he thought had called him. Three times this happened before Eli realised it must be God calling. He then said to Samuel, '... if he calls you, say, "Speak Lᴏʀᴅ, for your servant is listening."'

With all that Samuel had learnt over many years about God and the practicalities of serving him, he still did not know him. Can that happen today? I've met people who have heard God's voice audibly. I never have. Most times God speaks into our hearts and minds, but it can be difficult to know when it is God speaking to us or just our own thoughts.

Only as we come to know God more and more do we become familiar with his ways and voice. It was Paul's greatest desire. May it be ours too. *John 10:1-4, 14-15; Philippians 3:10*

PRAYER

Now my heart's desire is to know you more,
To be found in you and be known as yours...
(Graham Kendrick)[3]   *SASB* 565

Courage to obey

Samuel lay down until morning and then opened the doors of the house of the LORD. He was afraid to tell Eli the vision (v 15)

DOING what God would have us do can be very scary, more so for someone as young as Samuel. We love to share good news, positive tidings. What God told Samuel was his outright condemnation of both Eli and his family. No wonder Samuel was afraid to tell the old priest. Following his encounter with God, Samuel may well have laid down but I doubt he was able to sleep.

Have you ever felt convicted by God to deal with a situation, perhaps confront someone over an issue, and been so frightened to do so that you have lost sleep over the matter? It's not unusual. Some things take a great deal of prayer before we take action. It isn't just what we then do but also how we do it that matters.

Sometimes God provides us with help, as he did Samuel when Eli insisted that Samuel tell him everything, holding nothing back. I wonder how Eli felt with God speaking to a young boy rather directly with him? He was a priest – the religious professional, if you like – yet in all his years of service had God ever spoken personally to him? It was through another, 'a man of God', that Eli had received God's earlier message.

2:27-34

But Eli wasn't full of his own importance and was willing to listen to what that boy had to say. He was also ready to humbly recognise the truth of the matter and how God's judgement on him and his family was valid. At times we need to hear what we don't wish to hear and accept the unpalatable truth about ourselves. It's always the first step to getting right with God.

3:18

This was also the first example of the faith, courage and obedience that Samuel would display throughout his life.

PRAYER

O give me Samuel's ear, the open ear, O Lord,
Alive and quick to hear each whisper of thy word;
Like him to answer at thy call and to obey thee first
of all.

SASB 839 v 3
(1986 edition)

(James Drummond Burns)

Who is on the Lord's side?

'Why did the LORD bring defeat on us today before the Philistines?' (v 3)

THE Philistines had been gathering to wage war against the Israelites and the Israelites went out to fight them, only to be heavily defeated. They had expected God to give them victory and so considered him to be responsible for their defeat. How often have opposing armies each believed God to be on their side?

Knowing they were God's specially chosen people, the Israelites could not understand how they could have been defeated by such a pagan force. But rather than discover why God might not have given them victory, they sent men to Shiloh to bring back the Ark of the Covenant. The ark was the focal point of Israel's worship, representing God's presence among his people, but they used it like a talisman, believing it would guarantee God's presence and assure them of victory.

Its arrival was celebrated so loudly that the Philistines could hear the commotion. On discovering the reason for the noise and aware of what Israel's God was capable of, they were fearful. But their fear of becoming subservient to the Hebrews was even greater and so they were going to have to fight. However, the Israelites were in for a shock. Not only was their defeat heavier, but the Philistines captured their precious ark and Hophni and Phinehas were killed – as had been predicted.   2:34

How different things might have been if Israel had repented and sought God's mind on their predicament. They wanted God's blessing but not God's will. They were more concerned in having God on their side, thinking they could force his hand by bringing the ark into the situation rather than examining themselves to see if they were on God's side.

Do we ever make decisions we think best and then seek God's blessing on them rather than seek his will? Is it possible to revere religious rituals, objects, buildings and the like, yet be lacking in the essence of what it is all about?   2 Timothy 3:5

PRAYER
Father, purify my heart and motives. Make me more concerned with being on your side rather than you being on mine.

Singing in the night … when we realise our need of God

'Blessed are the poor in spirit, for theirs is the kingdom of heaven' (Matthew 5:3)

HOW well do you really know the Beatitudes? For the next few weekends we will be exploring them and the picture they paint of those who have found Jesus – those who live closely with him each day. If you want to explore further, Luke has a parallel shorter version, followed by a series of opposites (see Luke 6:20-26). But for now, let's begin with today's key verse.

The Greek word translated as 'blessed' or 'happy' (*makarios*) is an expression of congratulation. The person who is *makarios* is held up as a good example to be followed. Translators have struggled to find the most suitable English parallel.

Being 'poor in spirit' is not a phrase we use often today. What does it mean? *The Message* paraphrase suggests, 'You're blessed when you're at the end of your rope.' When life fragments, as happened for many during the coronavirus global pandemic for instance, we realise just how much we need God: his love; his reassurance; an awareness of his presence.

At times like that, the Holy Spirit shows us that there is much more to know of God – and also how much he longs to comfort us. Then we discover how 'spiritually poor' (*GNB*) we really are, and so we are drawn to seek his help in our difficulties.

That is when a new song can begin, one telling the depths of our need for God. Psalm 42 expresses such need, then moves into greater trust in him. Does it echo the feelings of your own heart? If so, pray the words of the psalm to him. He will certainly hear and understand.

Jesus says that when we realise the greatness of our need of him, the Kingdom of Heaven is ours. Or, as *The Message* paraphrase expresses it: 'With less of you there is more of God and his rule.' What a promise! Singing the song of those who realise their need of God opens the door to all he wants to give to us – *all* of it!

Ephesians 3:16-21 sums that up nicely for us. Take a moment to reflect on that passage also today.

... when we are grieving

'Blessed are those who mourn, for they will be comforted' (Matthew 5:4)

THERE has been so much grief and loss during the past two years. The coronavirus pandemic has torn families apart and broken lives. Loved ones have gone, jobs and essential income have been lost; personal freedom and social patterns on which we depend for quality of life have been affected. So much has changed – for all of us. We are grieving. The father of the prodigal son (spoken about by Jesus in Luke 15) must have grieved deeply too as he watched daily for the safe return of his wayward child.

But there is another kind of grief also, which we experience when we realise the enormity of our own sin: how it has hurt God, damaged others and tainted our personalities. *Then* we grieve over our loss of purity, goodness and self-respect – and loss of unhindered relationships with God and those around us. This step on the road to true repentance and salvation is important, underlining our determination to turn around and go God's way. The prodigal son made some progress along that road – to reach his father.

The Message paraphrases today's key verse: 'You're blessed when you feel you've lost what is most dear to you. Only then can you be embraced by the One most dear to you.' Grieving is to feel the loss of 'what is most dear'. Sometimes it makes us feel angry too. God is ready to hold us in our sadness and anger over lost loved ones, lost employment, lost freedom – and all other losses (see Revelation 7:17). And when our grief is the other kind – part of repentance – God is ready to embrace us and welcome us back into his family.

'How happy are those who know what sorrow means for they will be given courage and comfort!' (*JBP*) When we experience grief, we are promised courage as well as comfort. The word 'comfort', from Latin words *cum forte*, literally means 'with strength'. God stands with us; his Spirit strengthens us. We are not alone.

What song can we sing in our grief? Psalm 22:1-5 helped Jesus (see Matthew 27:45-46) and can help us too. You may like to use it now, to express your own prayers.

Bad news, sad news

'The Glory has departed from Israel' (vv 21 and 22)

HAVE you ever waited for news with both hope and fear: hoping for the best and fearing the worst? Such was our family's case while surgeons operated on my father following the serious injuries he received in a road accident. It has also been the case for so many people these past two years with loved ones in intensive care in hospital, fighting COVID-19.

Eli had not been able to prevent his sons taking the Ark of the Covenant to the Israelite frontline. Blind, and now 98 years old, there was little he could do other than sit at the city gate and await news of what had happened to it.

Anyone seeing the messenger from the battlefront arrive in Shiloh would have known from his appearance the nature of the news he was about to share. His clothes were torn and his head was covered with dust. Eli obviously didn't see him arrive at the gate but heard the uproar of the crowd as they were told what had happened.

When the man then told Eli how the Israelite army had been routed, his two sons killed and the ark captured, it was that final piece of news that hit him the hardest, rather than the deaths of his sons. His heart had 'feared for the ark', and this news broke his heart. He fell off his chair, broke his neck and died.

When the pregnant wife of Phinehas heard that her husband and father-in-law were dead and the ark captured, the shock sent her into labour. But the birth of her healthy baby boy brought her no joy, for she was dying. However, before she died she was able to give the child the name Ichabod, meaning 'no glory' – and she added: 'The Glory has departed from Israel.'

I can't help wondering if 'the Glory' had already departed before the ark was captured. Had its presence at Shiloh given everyone a false sense of security regarding God's presence and approval?

PRAYER

Father, hold my hand firmly in uncertain times, and may my faith be in you and you alone.

There is no other God

Then they carried the ark into Dagon's temple and set it beside Dagon (v 2)

THE Philistines, like most nations in and around Israel, had many gods and could happily add another to the gods they already had. Previously, they had been fearful of Israel's God, but having defeated the Israelites they concluded that Dagon was responsible for their victory and therefore more powerful.

4:7

Nevertheless, they treated the Ark of the Covenant with respect, placing it in Dagon's temple beside their revered idol: a place of honour for their trophy and a reminder of their triumph. But God can never accept being one among many: 'I am the Lord; that is my name! I will not yield my glory to another or my praise to idols.'

Isaiah 42:8

The Israelites had dishonoured God in their attempt to use him to achieve their own aims, whereas the Philistines didn't realise that in their effort to honour Israel's God they actually insulted him. Even with our best intentions, do we ever still get things wrong?

Returning to Dagon's temple the following morning, they discovered Dagon had fallen face down on the ground before the ark. The Philistines were not having that! They lifted it back in place, probably nailing it down so that it didn't topple, yet what sort of a god would need human help just to stand up? The following morning it had fallen again, and this time its head and arms were broken off. Was that the true God trying to show the Philistines Dagon's complete lack of wisdom and strength?

Isaiah 41:7

If only the Philistines had adopted the posture of their fallen idol, and humbled and prostrated themselves in repentance before the God of Israel, rejecting the absurdity of their religion, they may have saved themselves from God's wrath that followed. Instead of replacing Dagon with the ark, they hallowed the very threshold on which Dagon had fallen.

Is God alone on the throne and the very centre of our lives? Or have we loves that we will not concede to his sovereignty?

PRAYER
> The dearest idol I have known, whate'er that idol be,
> Help me to tear it from thy throne and worship
> only thee.

(William Cowper)   *SASB* 612 v 5

Even bad people are capable of good things

'Now then, get a new cart ready, with two cows that have calved and never been yoked. Hitch the cows to the cart, but take the calves away' (v 7)

IF only the Philistines had accepted the God of Israel as their own God, how different the story may well have been for them. But, as we found yesterday, they pushed him away, sending the ark of God from one city to another. What could have been a blessing became a curse, and after seven months they wanted rid of the ark for good.

Acknowledging they had offended Israel's God, the Philistine priests and diviners advised that the ark be returned to Israel together with a guilt offering. Only then would they know the healing of Israel's God.

God's people do not have a freehold on goodness. Even people generally considered 'bad' are capable of doing good.

Joshua 2

Rahab the prostitute is but one example. Jesus made the point that as bad as people may be, they know how to give

Matthew 7:11

their children good things.

Out of respect for Israel's God, the Philistines made a new cart for the ark, feeling that a cart previously used for common purposes was unworthy of such a task. To pull it they chose two cows, deliberately separated from their young calves and never having been yoked to pull a cart before. Untrained, inexperienced and with no driver guiding those cows, one would have expected them to stray off the road to feed themselves or turn back to find their calves. But they chose the right road and went straight to Beth Shemesh. The Philistines felt Israel's God had guided the cows, confirming to them that he was responsible for what they had been through.

Beth Shemesh was a town set aside for priests. They should

Numbers 4:20

have known not to open the ark and look inside. Those who did paid a high price. It is something the Philistines never did; they seemed more respectful of Israel's holy things than the Israelites were. Sometimes non-believers can reveal virtues absent in believers.

PRAYER

Father, give me the eyes to see good in others and the humility to acknowledge virtues lacking in me. Like those cows, may I be directed by you and not diverted by other concerns, attractions and temptations.

Returning to God

Then all the people ... turned back to the LORD (v 2)

I GAVE my heart to Jesus when I was just seven years old. He was very real to me and I wanted others to know and experience what I had found. In my early teens I felt drawn towards ministry as an officer in The Salvation Army. But sadly, moral lapses among people I admired as role models shocked, disappointed and discouraged me, and I took my eyes off Jesus and withdrew my application for ministry.

I continued to attend The Salvation Army but the joy had left me and eventually I left. However, although I had given up on God, God never gave up on me. He broke through my foolish, stubborn resistance one evening when I was 30 years old and I returned to him.

Under Eli's 40-year leadership, characterised by his unwillingness to deal with bad issues, Israel's religious life degenerated through neglect and misuse of the things of God. Though God was patient, the final straw came when the Ark of the Covenant was taken into battle like some lucky charm in the hope of ensuring the nation's victory. The subsequent defeat and capture of the ark stunned the nation.

Although they rejoiced when the ark was returned, the people of Beth Shemesh (predominantly priests) had learnt little regarding reverence for the majesty and awesomeness of God – possibly the influence of Eli's sons over decades. They treated the ark with familiarity and disrespect, something God was not prepared to tolerate any more. Verse 19 tells how swift and severe his response was.

Yet God had not given up on the nation. He still wanted a relationship with Israel. But it had to be on his terms. God's response to their behaviour shocked the people and made them aware of just how awesome and powerful was 'this holy God'. In time, all the people would turn back to God.

Do we treat God and come before him in worship with the reverence and awe we ought?

PRAYER

We praise you, God, for ever loving us and never giving up on any of us – even though we fail and disappoint you.

The battle is the Lord's

... saying, 'Thus far the LORD has helped us' (v 12)

IT had been more than seven months since Eli died. Samuel, already recognised throughout the nation as 'a prophet of the LORD', was Eli's natural successor as leader and judge. Shiloh was now desolate, no longer the nation's religious centre. The Ark of the Covenant never returned there, but was taken to Abinadab's house in Kiriath Jearim, where it remained until King David removed it 46 years later.

3:20
Jeremiah 7:12-15

1 Chronicles
13:5-14

Following 20 years of Samuel's ministry, the nation turned back to the Lord with Samuel insisting they prove their sincerity by ridding themselves of all their idols. They were to serve God alone. Our true desires and intentions are always confirmed by our actions. The whole nation responded positively to Samuel's unequivocal message, enabling him to intercede with God on their behalf.

He then summoned all the people to Mizpah. In humility, the people drew water and poured it on the ground, indicating their helpless position before God. For as water poured on the ground cannot be recovered, neither can the sins we have committed be undone. The whole nation fasted and confessed their sins while Samuel brought them to God in prayer.

2 Samuel 14:14

Suddenly, aware that the Philistine army was approaching, the people, full of fear, pleaded with Samuel not to stop praying for them. In response, he offered a sacrifice and cried out to God. God answered by sending thunder loud enough to terrorise the Philistines, throwing them all into panic. The Israelites then pursued them, destroying their army.

To commemorate the victory, Samuel set up a stone which he named Ebenezer – meaning 'stone of help' – a reminder of what God had done for the people. Peace reigned.

We may not know our future but it isn't something to be feared. If we have placed our well-being in God's hands we will have experienced his providential care in the past and know we can trust him with what lies ahead.

TO PONDER

Through many dangers, toils and snares I have
    already come;
'Tis grace has brought me safe thus far and grace will
    lead me Home.   (John Newton)

SASB 453 v 3

Singing in the night ... when we live by God's values

'Blessed are the meek, for they will inherit the earth' (Matthew 5:5)

WHAT do you do when someone challenges or offends you, taunts you or puts you down? Are you meek? It depends on what 'meek' means, perhaps. If it is to be 'quiet, gentle, and always ready to do what other people want without expressing your own opinion',[4] that sounds like being a doormat; allowing others to walk all over you. Jesus called himself 'meek' (Matthew 11:29 *KJV*) but he did not usually give in to others like that. The Greek words used in both today's key verse and in Matthew 11 translate into English as 'easy, mild', so what else may 'meek' mean?

Meekness has been described as 'the ability to control one's power and use it only for the benefit of others'.[5] So, a meek person can express anger appropriately: the opposite of being a doormat!

Human nature instinctively draws us to use our abilities and strengths to further our own causes; to use conflict for our own advantage. Worldly values say, 'Fight for your own interests; push yourself forward; don't worry about treading on another's toes.' In contrast, the meek respond with the values of Jesus, for the benefit of others rather than themselves.

So, is meekness forcing ourselves to act or respond in certain ways while inwardly seething? No! Clearly, we cannot be truly meek without God.

Some wrongly regard true meekness as weakness. Jesus was misunderstood in that way during his trial (see Luke 23:8-11). When we entrust to God our powers, abilities, feelings and responses, we can remain unruffled by circumstances. Then the whole earth is open to us; with God, nothing is impossible (see Mark 10:27; Luke 1:37).

We saw last Saturday that to be 'poor in spirit', to realise how deeply we need God, makes all the resources of Heaven available to us (see Matthew 5:3). As we draw upon them, we find that the whole earth is open to us too; anything is possible. God enables us to face each challenging situation in *his* way, with love, gentle firmness and quiet confidence in him.

When living by God's values becomes a challenge, Psalm 27:1-6 may be the song to sing. Try it today.

... when we long to be more like Jesus

'Blessed are those who hunger and thirst for righteousness, for they will be filled' (Matthew 5:6)

WHEN did you last feel desperately hungry or thirsty – so hungry or thirsty that you became too weak to function normally? We saw last Saturday that Matthew 5:3 speaks of a deep need for God in daily living. Today's Beatitude takes us to another level: a desire for more and more of God; a desperate longing to become more *like* him.

Sometimes the Holy Spirit makes us aware of how little we really know God; how much more there is to know; how much deeper our relationship with him can be. It's rather like mountain climbing: when we near the top we see higher peaks beyond which we could not see lower down – and where the view is even more amazing.

This can happen especially when we look closely at Jesus and then at ourselves – and see the vast difference between us and him. Jesus shows us the nature of God. God's love, purity, selflessness and justice shine through every action, word and decision of Jesus. Matthew 5:6 does imply hungering and thirsting for more of God, a deeper relationship with him, but also hungering and thirsting for 'righteousness' – an insatiable longing to *become* more like him.

Further still, it is also a deep longing for God's goodness and justice to be seen not only in us but in all who have received him by faith – and in the whole world.

We are promised that our deep longings to be more like Jesus will be satisfied. As we look at him through his Word, gaze steadily at who he is – and the painful contrasts between him and us – he has promised to meet our longing with his grace. As we spend time with him and let him take the lead each day, as his Spirit lives within us more and more fully, we *will* become more like Jesus.

What is our 'song in the night' when we desperately long to be more like God, as seen in Jesus? Psalm 51:1-17 expresses that longing. If it is your longing too, try telling Jesus now through the words of this psalm-song.

Be careful what you ask for

'...appoint a king to lead us, such as all the other nations have' (v 5)

SAMUEL worked hard over a number of years travelling the country on a regular circuit as its judge. But his labours and the years took their toll, with him needing to delegate many of his responsibilities.

There may have been better candidates for Samuel to choose, but he chose his sons as Israel's leaders. While Joel and Abijah were not as bad as Eli's sons, they were dishonest, more concerned with making money than dispensing justice. Perhaps none of this was apparent until they were put into positions of responsibility and opportunity. Some people's behaviour changes to reveal their hearts only once restraints are lifted.

Much concerned, the elders of Israel requested that Samuel appoint a king 'such as all the other nations have'. In other words, they wanted to be like other countries with all the grandeur, pomp and display that a prophet lacked. The world is often more concerned with and impressed by appearances than unseen realities.

Israel was a theocracy: God was Israel's king and led the nation through its priests. Samuel was of that priestly order. Deeply troubled and feeling rejected, Samuel brought his grief to God, who made it clear that it wasn't Samuel but God they were rejecting. He then told Samuel to listen to what they had to say before warning them of the consequences of God granting their request.

1 Chronicles 6:33-48

Although Samuel described the oppression a king would bring, something Israel would experience by the end of King Solomon's reign, the elders persisted in their request and so God told Samuel to let them have what they wanted.

see 1 Kings 12:4

If we persist in seeking what *we* want or feel is best, God may reluctantly let us have it – together with the consequences of our choice! Let us be careful what we ask for. God did not desire Israel to be like other nations: we too are called to be a people different from those who do not live under his sovereignty.

PRAYER
Help me to align my requests to what you desire, Lord God, and make me willing to be different, set apart, living solely for your glory.

Thank God for good companions

The servant answered him again. 'Look,' he said, 'I have a quarter of a shekel of silver. I will give it to the man of God...' (v 8)

see v 20

MOST handsome of men, Saul stood much taller than anyone else in Israel. He came from a good family, his father being highly regarded, and he was an obedient, considerate son. Having been asked to find his father's lost donkeys, Saul and one of his father's servants spent three days travelling from place to place in their search.

Although they took food with them the search took much longer than expected and, with the food gone and concern that his father would now be worrying about them rather than the donkeys, Saul decided they needed to get back home. However, the servant was aware of a 'man of God' nearby who might help them and persuaded Saul to seek him out.

What a critical moment that was! No doubt they were both tired and hungry. Who would have blamed Saul had he ignored his servant's suggestion and headed home – but he didn't. Praise God for the times he gives us a companion who guides us in the right direction when, for good reasons, we might easily have taken some other path.

8:4

But Saul was concerned at not having anything to give the 'man of God' – Samuel, of course. That might not have been because Samuel expected or required anything for his services, but that Saul wanted to show his respect and gratitude to this godly man. Today, when someone invites us for a meal, don't we naturally like to take a gift of some kind to our host?

The servant then offered the quarter of a shekel he had in his possession. God loves us, his children, to be sacrificial givers; it is a reflection of the character of God himself. That servant was willing to sacrifice all that he had, when he could have kept it to himself. Saul possibly would have been none the wiser. Without his servant's generous spirit Saul may have given up the idea of approaching Samuel and gone back home.

PRAYER
Father, thank you for those companions who have ensured I take the right path when I may have so easily chosen another.

When someone else is preferred

'... And to whom is all the desire of Israel turned, if not to you' (v 20)

SAUL and his companion approached the town of Ramah just as a group of young women were coming down the hill to draw water. It would have been in the cool of early evening, a practice centuries old. They confirmed Samuel was in town but that Saul would need to hurry as Samuel was preparing to go and bless the sacrifice the people were waiting to eat. Samuel had built an altar at Ramah, further up the hill from the town – 'the high place' mentioned in verse 12.

Genesis 24:11, 13

7:17

God informed Samuel the previous day that Saul was coming and was the one he was to anoint as king. Was it Saul who told Samuel about his father's lost donkeys or did God tell him that too? One of the wonders of God is that he is equally concerned about the ordinary things in our individual lives as he is big dramatic issues. I'm always amazed that, having seen their daughter raised from the dead, it was Jesus rather than Jairus and his wife who thought of the girl's need of food.

see Mark 5:40-43

8:6-8

Despite feeling rejected and having to make way for this mere farm worker to succeed him as the nation's leader, Samuel showed no resentment towards him. He was nothing but a blessing and encouragement to Saul, honouring him by walking behind him to the meal and giving him the top seat and best food. Is that how we are towards someone we think to be less qualified or deserving than ourselves when they receive preferential treatment? I wonder if Samuel still had feelings of hurt.

One of our biggest dangers is allowing what we feel to govern our actions or reactions, while one of the hardest things for Christians is to have the 'me' in us crucified, so that with Paul we can say, 'I have been crucified with Christ and I no longer live, but Christ lives in me.'

Galatians 2:20

PRAYER

Lord Jesus, help me not to be jealous or resent someone who is preferred to me when I feel I'm more deserving or worthy. May I be gracious and genuine in my goodwill towards them.

Transformed by the Spirit

'The Spirit of the Lord will come powerfully upon you ... and you will be changed into a different person' (v 6)

UP at daybreak despite what was probably a late night talking together on the roof of Samuel's house, Saul got ready to return home. As he, his servant and Samuel reached the edge of town, Samuel wanted to share a private message from God with Saul. Sending the servant ahead, Samuel administered God's anointing of Saul as king. In addition, that dear old man of God kissed him, a sign of his own personal allegiance. What a wonderful heart he had towards Saul!

Samuel then predicted three things Saul would experience on his way home, a confirmation this was all of God. First, Saul would discover that his father had stopped thinking about the donkeys and was worrying about him, just as he had feared.

9:5

Next, as Saul approached his home town of Gibeah he would meet a procession of prophets playing musical instruments and prophesying, and the Spirit of the Lord would come down powerfully upon him. He would join them in prophesying and 'be changed into a different person'.

9:21

Saul was untrained, ill-equipped and the least likely man to lead a nation – and he knew it. But the Spirit of God would turn this humble farmer's son into a gifted commander of men with the confidence, capacity and disposition to be God's king.

Samuel's final word was a command. Saul was to go down to Gilgal, wait there seven days and do nothing until Samuel arrived to offer sacrifices. Samuel would tell Saul what he was

see 13:11-14

to do. His response to this command would prove his undoing.

We too might feel inadequate, ill-equipped and incapable of the role God has for us. He loves choosing the most unlikely people before transforming them. By his Spirit God can turn us into very different people, giving us what we lack. We then need to act with confidence in God, putting our hand to the task the Lord gives us.

PRAYER

Father, I am incapable of being and doing what you desire of me. Send your Holy Spirit with power to transform me into the person you wish me to be.

Fear of the future

... And the Lᴏʀᴅ said, 'Yes, he has hidden himself among the supplies' (v 22)

SAUL'S heart changed as he left Samuel. No longer was his heart narrowly focused on the things about his father's farm; it was enlarged, encompassing the things of national importance that he would be responsible for.

As Saul neared home he met the procession of prophets, as Samuel forecast, and joined them in prophesying. Neighbours who knew him watched on and were amazed at what they witnessed. They began wondering what had happened to Saul. When he finished prophesying Saul went to the sacred high place, probably to thank God for all he had experienced.

When his inquisitive uncle asked where he had been, all Saul would say was that he had been looking for the donkeys and Samuel had helped him find them. Was it humility or prudence that prevented Saul from telling his uncle everything that had happened? Sometimes it is wise to remain silent regarding what we know or what the Lord has told us. It's certainly never wise or right to proclaim ourselves.

Samuel then called all Israel to Mizpah to present Saul as their king, having first reminded them of all God had done for them – and how they had rejected God in demanding a king. He had them choose their king by lot, a process God would control as he had already chosen Saul. However, when all but Saul's name had been eliminated he was nowhere to be seen. He may have been well hidden from people but he could not hide from God.

Why did Saul hide himself, we may well ask. Probably for the same reason that you and I might hide from a daunting task that takes us out of our comfort zone – fear! Fear of failure, fear of other people's envy, fear of the crowd, fear that some might not accept him.

On finding Saul, Samuel presented their new king to the people. Most were delighted, but there were those who despised him. However, verse 27 tells us: 'Saul kept silent.' God would verify his choice.

PRAYER
When fear would seize me and have me hide away, Lord, give me the courage and faith in you which I lack.

Singing in the night ... when we need to respond in love

'Blessed are the merciful, for they will be shown mercy' (Matthew 5:7)

DURING the early days of the coronavirus pandemic in the United Kingdom we were encouraged to stand outside our houses on Thursday evenings and clap for all who were helping to relieve suffering and maintain essential services. Some of us even played musical instruments or beat metal pots and pans to accompany the applause! We were showing appreciation for those who were placing their own lives in danger on our behalf. Those workers were expressing mercy.

Mercy demonstrates loving care towards any who are suffering physically, mentally, emotionally or spiritually. Mercy can also be 'a loving response to an offender who may or may not realise their offence.'[6] This expression of mercy includes forgiveness (see Matthew 18:21-33).

Both forms of mercy require time, effort and an awareness of the other person's situation. Showing mercy takes us out of ourselves. When we are offended, we instinctively focus on our own hurt and anger. Reaching beyond that, to the offender's need of our forgiveness, does not come naturally. We need God's help: his love and grace. Similarly, helping someone in need requires us to put aside our own agenda and plans for that moment, like the Good Samaritan in Luke 10:30-37.

Jesus promises that when we do this, with his help, we ourselves will receive mercy in return. How does that work? Is God more merciful to those who show mercy? Well, not necessarily. God's love and grace are there for us all, always. Perhaps we just become more able to receive his love and grace when we have opened our own hearts to others.

When we hold ourselves aloof from the problems of others, we close our hearts and become unable to receive all that God wants to give us. Or to say it another way, when our hands are closed tightly upon all that we treasure, there is no more room in our hands to receive anything else, including God's love and mercy.

We need God's help here: his love to grow in our hearts, his eyes to see the needs of others. The song of Lamentations 3:19-26 may help us to open hearts and hands to others – in his name.

... when our lifestyle is different

'Blessed are the pure in heart, for they will see God' (Matthew 5:8)

LIFESTYLES? There are so many! Social media 'influencers' promote particular ways of living; news reports and advertisements present us with many more. We are urged to 'be ourselves'.

Only one lifestyle really matters when we belong to Jesus: being like him; living by his standards; following his lead. When 'being ourselves' actually means becoming like Jesus, this is a huge challenge. To be different, to stand out as his follower, can invite opposition or even rejection. Being like Jesus includes being 'pure in heart'. Pure hearts produce pure thoughts, pure speech, pure actions – and that can offend others when it contrasts with their own lifestyles.

'Two men looked out from prison bars. One saw mud, the other saw stars.'[7] Each of us looks at life differently. When our hearts are pure, we begin to see with God's eyes: we see the best, the possibilities, the good. Why is this? Perhaps because when we have been cleansed in heart and mind, we see more clearly who God is and how he sees this world – and in seeing we come closer to him; become more like him.

The Holy Spirit longs to deal with the uncleanness which accumulates in our minds and hearts: the prejudice, hidden anger, resentment, bitterness and impure thoughts which colour our judgements. It is a refining process (see Zechariah 13:9; Malachi 3:3). Gold is purified by strong heat, so that the impure particles rise to the surface and can be removed. The Holy Spirit's cleansing is similar. He can show us the impure things within, helping us to acknowledge them and release them to him.

Then we can begin to see as God sees: see what he is like; see his hand at work in those around us; see the changes he brings to our own minds, hearts and lives. 'You're blessed when you get your inside world – your mind and heart – put right. Then you can see God in the outside world' (v 8 *MSG*).

Psalm 139:1-12, 23-24 sings of how deeply God knows us – and of our desire for him to purify us. Why not pray this psalm just now?

The interests of others

When Saul heard their words, the Spirit of God came powerfully upon him, and he burned with anger (v 6)

ACCORDING to the Dead Sea Scrolls, Nahash, King of Ammon, terrorised the tribes of Reuben and Gad, which bordered Ammon. He gouged out their right eyes, but 7,000 survivors managed to escape to the relative safety of Jabesh Gilead. Nahash then besieged the town and would only agree to a treaty that allowed him to gouge out the right eyes of everyone in it. He was not interested in plundering the town or them paying tribute; he wanted Israel ridiculed, humiliated.

Deuteronomy 3:12-20

Before he died Moses divided the land of Canaan between the tribes. Gad, Reuben and half the tribe of Manasseh were given territory on the eastern side of the River Jordan, with the command that they cross the Jordan and help their fellow Israelites take possession of their lands before settling in their own. When Joshua reminded them of Moses' command, they obeyed.

Joshua 1:12-15

Once settled, the tribes became more insular; local interests took precedence over the common good with no unified national response to any tribe's crisis. Whether one tribe helped another depended on the closeness of the danger to them. Support from other tribes could never be guaranteed. Consequently, Nahash was so confident that help would not be forthcoming from tribes the other side of the Jordan that he allowed messengers to go throughout the land appealing for it.

When news reached Saul, the Spirit of the Lord descended on him and he was furious. With concern for his fellow Israelites and the nation's honour, Saul sent out a call to arms throughout Israel, with a warning to anyone who failed to respond. As a result, 330,000 men came together under King Saul's leadership and they obliterated the Ammonite army, liberating Jabesh Gilead.

Philippians 2:4
RSV see also
Matthew 22:39

The apostle Paul wrote, 'Let each of you look not only to his own interests, but also to the interests of others', a message of love in contrast to those Israelite tribes that were motivated by fear or self-interest.

PRAYER

Father, give me a heart that responds out of love to the needs of others in the same way as I attend to my own needs.

Bless those who curse you

But Saul said, 'No one will be put to death today, for this day the Lord has rescued Israel' (v 13)

KING Saul revealed a hitherto hidden gift of leadership in galvanising the whole nation to respond to Jabesh Gilead's need, mustering a huge army and marching them nearly 60 miles to a resounding victory over the Ammonites. It convinced those who were uncertain and those who thought him totally unsuitable for the role that the right man had been chosen as king.

With no festivities when Samuel presented Saul as king, the fickle people now sensed greatness in their midst and celebrated. People who never voiced it before called for vengeance on those who had shown contempt for Saul. Some people wait to see which way the wind is blowing before they voice an opinion, and those now demanding the death of the men who had previously despised Saul may well have despised him themselves had the battle been lost and Saul humiliated. *10:25*

10:27

Saul remained silent when insulted; he didn't desire revenge on a day of joy and celebration. God had been good to Saul and he was not going to be unmerciful towards those who had opposed him. *see Matthew 18:21-35*

It was Jesus who said, 'Love your enemies, do good to those who hate you, bless those who curse you, pray for those who ill-treat you.' That is not easy, but it is the first step in making a friend of an enemy. It is also an aspect of God's own character. Saul's magnanimity may well have resulted in an allegiance to him which was absent before. *Luke 6:27-28* *Romans 5:10; Colossians 1:21-22*

A very unpleasant woman lived in a flat a few doors from my friend. Although she tried being friendly, the woman made a point of being rude whenever they met. It distressed my friend: she dreaded stepping outside her door. While praying one day she felt convinced she was to buy a big bouquet and leave it with a note outside the woman's door. It melted the ice and the nasty neighbour knocked on her door in tears. It was the beginning of reconciliation and friendship.

PRAYER
Lord, give me a forgiving heart of goodwill towards those who show me ill will.

Growing old

'Now you have a king as your leader. As for me, I am old and grey ...' (v 2)

HAVING concluded worship in a care home one Sunday morning, I was informed by a carer that an elderly couple would like to speak to me in private. We met in a side room. The woman was in a wheelchair and her husband sat beside her with his walking frame alongside his chair.

'Sorry to bother you, but we wondered whether you would be willing to conduct our funerals,' the wife asked. 'Have you a date in mind?' I replied, provoking uncontrolled laughter from the two of them.

As a result of our brief conversation I visited them regularly. They were both well into their nineties and had been much involved in a church in town, but had not heard from anyone there for years. They felt they had been cast aside now that they were no longer deemed useful.

8:22

7:13-14

Samuel had listened to the people and given them the king they asked for, as God told him to. Throughout Samuel's lifetime God had subdued the Philistines, and captured territory had been restored to Israel. However, as he grew old Samuel recognised his inability to do all he once did and appointed his sons to help. But sadly they turned out to be corrupt.

8:5

In demanding a king like other nations, the elders of Israel rejected both Samuel and the way in which he had governed Israel for decades. He took it very personally, as today's passage reveals, asking them whether they doubted his integrity. The people assured him that wasn't the case.

Psalm 71:9, 12

Isaiah 46:4

Regrettably, many Christians feel cast aside when they reach old age. The world often values people according to what they can give, abandoning them when they can no longer give and need to receive. Sadder still is when, following a lifetime of service, this happens in the Church. Despite fears to the contrary, God doesn't forsake his people in old age: 'Even to your old age and grey hairs ... I am he who will sustain you.'

PRAYER

Father, although they may no longer be able to do what once they did or even attend church, may the elderly never feel cast aside, unvalued or neglected. Show us how to show them they are still precious.

God never gives up on us

'For the sake of his great name the LORD will not reject his people, because the LORD was pleased to make you his own' (v 22)

SOMETIMES we can do something we come to regret, with consequences that we cannot reverse. We wish we could go back to where we were and start again. But we can't, and we wonder if God will ever be able to forgive us. This was the situation facing the Israelites when they realised the enormity of their sin in demanding God give them a king.

Samuel's condemnation of what the people had asked for could have been dismissed by them as mere words, or a resentful response to his being rejected as their leader. Or they may have thought that Saul's victory and their celebration and sacrifices (which we read about on Tuesday) had put the matter behind them with little harm done.

Either way, the people needed to realise just how displeased God was with them and that Samuel's words truly were from God. So, Samuel called on God to reveal the seriousness of what they had done by sending thunder and rain – something very rare at that time of year. It came that very day. Awestruck and humbled, the people called on Samuel to pray for their forgiveness.

While God would not retract his anointing of the king or the subsequent consequences of their choice, revealed later in their history, he had not given up on them. A king, though less see 31 January likely than a prophet, could live in obedience to God; and if the king and God's people did so, Samuel told them, all would be well. But if not … Verse 15 gives us the woeful outcome.

Having taken the wrong road and found ourselves in a worse place because we disobeyed him, God can create a new road. Though different to that which he originally planned for us, it will be just as good and fruitful. We may have to live with regrets and some consequences of our sin, but our loving Father isn't into giving up on his children or giving them second best.

PRAYER
I cannot get over just how wonderful, patient, loving and forgiving you are, Father. Help me to reveal my gratitude in the way I live the life you have given me.

'Pray for those who mistreat you'

'As for me, far be it from me that I should sin against the LORD by failing to pray for you' (v 23)

IT was Frederick Coutts, the eighth General of The Salvation Army, who spoke of there being 'no discharge in this war'. While we may retire from secular employment or from the payroll, and perhaps the responsibilities placed on us by our church, a true man or woman of God can never retire from serving God and ministering to people in some form.

Although no longer a judge and Israel's leader, Samuel continued in the service of his God and in ministering to the people of Israel. He would go on teaching people what was good and right, although idolatry would continue to threaten the people's wholehearted faithful service.

Does it do so today? What modern-day idols might there be that discourage and tempt God's people to serve God less than wholeheartedly? Samuel suggested that it would help the people if they focused on the great things God had done for them. Do we sometimes forget the great things God has done for us?

Even though we love the Lord, none of us is without sin. Is there a day that passes without us sinning in one way or another? What Samuel condemned was a persistence in doing evil, a persistence that lacked conscience, confession or desire to change.

1 John 1:8-9

When the people confessed their sin they asked Samuel to pray for them and Samuel said it would be a sin for him not to.

v 19

Luke 6:28

Jesus' command to 'pray for those who mistreat you' is far from easy. Samuel knew nothing of Jesus' words, yet he instinctively knew it would be wrong not to pray for the people who had mistreated him.

In Jesus and Stephen, the first Christian martyr, we see wonderful examples: 'Then Jesus said, "Father, forgive them, for they know not what they do"'; 'Then he [Stephen] fell on his knees and cried out, "Lord, do not hold this sin against them."'

Luke 23:34 *KJV*

Acts 7:60

PRAYER

Jesus, teach me how to pray like you for those who wish me ill or have done me harm.

Singing in the night ... when we are faced with conflict

'Blessed are the peacemakers, for they will be called children of God' (Matthew 5:9)

CONFLICT seems to be all around us these days: in the news; on social media; within families, employment situations, politics and many other places. Technology has opened to us new forms of connecting with each other and brought ease of information like never before. Sadly, it also exposes hidden conflicts – and can create more too. Internet trolls seek to cause pain, anger and division. What a bleak picture!

The disciples heard Jesus' words at a time of political, national and religious conflict: Roman versus Jew; Jew versus Samaritan (see John 4:9 for instance). His words must have startled them, especially when their natural instinct was to fight back (Luke 9:51-56; John 18:10-11). There was conflict even between the disciples (Mark 10:35-45).

Faced with conflict, how can we be peacemakers? Well, we could launch ourselves physically between opposing individuals or groups: occasionally that has to happen, to restore immediate peace until the matter can be settled more permanently. It does risk both sides turning against us though – and complicating the conflict further.

The Message paraphrases today's verse as: 'You're blessed when you can show people how to cooperate instead of compete or fight.' The challenge is huge. Great understanding, patience and impartiality is needed: the gentle strength of meekness (see Mark 10:42-44).

Jesus said that when we are peacemakers we will be known as children of God. Why is this? Perhaps because people will see in us something different: the desire to reconcile and to spread love instead of conflict. And, after all, peace is a hallmark of God and his Kingdom. Isaiah painted that picture (11:6-9). Jesus gave his peace to his disciples (John 14:27). So, being peacemakers we help to demonstrate what God and his Kingdom are like.

When we are people of peace ourselves, our very presence may calm a situation. However, if sometimes we ourselves create conflict, others will disregard our peacemaking attempts. We need the Spirit of Jesus living in us to make us more like him, producing peace and self-control (see Galatians 5:22-23).

Do you feel the need of this today? Try Isaiah's song in today's passage from chapter 26.

... when we suffer because of Jesus

'Blessed are those who are persecuted because of righteousness ... Blessed are you when people insult you, persecute you and falsely say all kinds of evil against you because of me' (Matthew 5:10-11)

HAVE you ever felt victimised because you love Jesus? Hungering and thirsting to be more like him (v 6) can incite opposition. As we live under the guidance of Jesus, lifestyle differences between us and others will show (see 6 February reflection), making us vulnerable to being belittled, undermined, bullied and slandered (2 Timothy 3:10-12).

It can mean missing promotion because we will not follow underhand practices, or ridiculed when we will not join in ribald conversation – or even when we order a soft drink! And social media's attack on anyone who is 'different' is deeply hurtful. Persecution can be like water torture, drip by drip gouging away at our confidence or even our faith. We may want to shout, 'How long, LORD?' (Psalm 13:1-2).

Of course, we can bring persecution on ourselves through pride if we present ourselves as better than those around us. A religious superiority complex is precisely the opposite of Jesus. If we are persecuted for that, we have only ourselves to blame; it is nothing of Jesus.

Jesus tells us to 'rejoice and be glad' when we suffer for him. Why? Because we are not alone: 'all heaven applauds' (v 12 *MSG*) – and because we begin to understand his suffering for us a little better (Philippians 3:7-11). 'You're blessed when your commitment to God provokes persecution. The persecution drives you even deeper into God's kingdom' (v 10 *MSG*).

Should we actively seek persecution then, making ourselves so super-saintly that others will feel goaded into taunting us? No! A persecution complex also does not honour Jesus. This is not about seeking persecution as a route to Heaven; it is about seeking to be like Jesus. That may result in persecution but it will be because Jesus is seen in us, not because of anything we create ourselves.

The 'song in the night' expressed in Psalm 22 is a huge encouragement. We reflected on verses 1-5 on 23 January. It ends in victory and praise. Perhaps that is why Jesus used it on the cross. Or if you need a shorter song for when persecution happens, try Psalm 13.

Trust and obey

'You have done a foolish thing,' Samuel said. 'You have not kept the command the LORD your God gave you...' (v 13)

SAUL decided to retain only 3,000 of his 330,000 fighting men following his victory at Jabesh Gilead. The audacious attack Jonathan then made on the Philistine outpost at Geba with 1,000 of them provoked the Philistines into doing something to put an end to what they saw as Israel's growing confidence and possible threat to Philistine domination of the region. See 7 February

As the Philistines advanced towards Michmash Saul retreated from the city. On arriving there the Philistines made it their base and amassed a huge military presence in readiness to crush Saul.

For some reason Saul's summons lacked the enthusiastic response that his previous one had, and many who did respond fled on hearing of the growing strength of the Philistine forces. Those who remained were terrified.

Samuel told Saul to wait seven days for him to come, sacrifice burnt offerings and tell him what he was to do. When Samuel didn't arrive that seventh day, Saul's remaining men began deserting him. So Saul took it upon himself to sacrifice the offerings, only for Samuel to arrive just as Saul finished. He was shocked at what he found: 10:8

- Saul planned to engage the Philistines without Samuel's guidance. He was self-reliant.
- He tried to force God's hand, taking on the sacred role of a priest.
- He allowed his feelings to override his better judgement and conscience.
- He made excuses rather than express regret and repentance.
- He lacked any conscience in gladly greeting Samuel on his arrival.

Saul's lack of trust and obedience would cost him dearly. We can best express our love for the Lord by our constant trust and obedience. 1 John 5:2-3

PRAYER
When the future looks hopeless and darkness descends, help me never to do the foolish thing, but to trust and obey you, Lord.

We are no match for the enemy

So on the day of the battle not a soldier with Saul and Jonathan had a sword or spear in his hand; only Saul and his son Jonathan had them (v 22)

HAVING condemned Saul for his foolishness and sin, disappointed and unhappy, Samuel left Saul and made his way to Gibeah, Saul's home town. With confidence gone and lacking Samuel's support, Saul and his decimated army of some 600 men followed Samuel to the relative safety of that same hill town.

The Philistines were skilled in making iron tools and weapons. The Israelites on the other hand were still in the Bronze Age. Their bronze weapons were no match for the Philistines' weapons of iron. Unwilling to share knowledge or resources with the Israelites, the Philistines also ensured there was not a blacksmith left in Israel. Their only concession was that of allowing Israelites to bring their farming implements to them for sharpening – albeit at a price. They were probably implements the Israelites were forced to purchase from them in the first place!

Although our passage closes with how the Israelites, other than Saul and Jonathan, had neither spear nor sword, the writer probably meant neither spear nor sword made of iron. They must have had weapons other than clubs and slings when they fought the Ammonites, and would surely have retrieved the weapons of the dead as well as those abandoned by their fleeing enemy.

Using Michmash as their base for what may have been a considerable length of time, the Philistines sent out devastating raiding parties with no fear of resistance from Saul. Basically, they overran the country. The situation looked hopeless for the Israelites.

We too are weak, unable to offer much resistance to the power and subtlety of our enemy, Satan. But God reminds us in his Word: "'Not by might nor by power, but by my Spirit,' says the LORD Almighty', adding that the mighty mountain will be

Zechariah 4:6-7   reduced to level ground. And Paul encourages us to put on the
Ephesians 6:10-18 whole armour of God; our strength is found in the Lord and
see also Psalm 121 his mighty power.

PRAYER

Father, help me not to rely on my gifts and abilities, but to recognise my weakness, inadequacy and helplessness, and my need to rely on you.

With God nothing is impossible

'... Perhaps the LORD will act on our behalf...' (v 6)

SAUL'S God-given purpose was to deliver Israel from the Philistines, but he was at a loss and stayed with his men in the safety of Gibeah while the Philistines did as they pleased, sending out raiding parties to harass, kill and oppress the people unchecked.

9:16

Aware that his 600 men stood no chance against the Philistine's military machine, Saul had not included God in his thinking. Here, when he should have done something, he waited; whilst earlier – as we read on Monday – when he should have waited, he acted.

What a different man Jonathan was! He was surely far more suited to be Israel's king than his father. God-focused, Jonathan had a great faith and was willing to attempt the impossible should God desire it. Verse 6 shows he didn't believe superiority in numbers was necessary for God to give victory. Had he heard of what God did with Gideon?

Judges ch 7

What would be deemed impossible for 600 men would be considered madness for just two. No wonder Jonathan kept his plan secret and only shared what he had in mind with his faithful armour-bearer who accompanied him. The Philistine outpost they intended to attack was on a cliff guarding the pass to the Philistine camp at Michmash. It meant a difficult climb for Jonathan and his companion.

It can be really difficult at times to know God's will and whether the powerful feeling that we must do something in response to a great concern we have comes from him, despite our prayers for guidance and confirmation. Although Jonathan knew God wanted Israel delivered from the Philistines, and he desired it too, he wasn't absolutely sure that what he was doing was God ordained. '*Perhaps* the LORD will act on our behalf,' he said. Only as they neared the top of the cliff did that confirmation come.

Isn't that often the way with you and me? We pray about an issue with a compulsion to do something and yet, stepping out in faith, we still lack certainty. Only as we continue do we realise that God is directing our paths.

Proverbs 3:6

PRAYER
Lord, when I step out in faith help me to trust you – despite my uncertainties.

The battle is the Lord's

So on that day the Lord saved Israel... (v 23)

JONATHAN and his armour-bearer had clambered up the cliff using both their hands and feet. They must have been breathless and weary when they got to the top. Yet, against all odds they were not overpowered by the Philistines but went on the offensive and killed 20 of them.

A panic sent by God ensued and spread from the outpost to the whole of the Philistine army. God speaks to the heart and can bring both peace and panic. The panic was increased by an earthquake that he, who created and controls nature, sent.

From their clifftop position Saul's lookouts could see and possibly hear the tumult across the valley. Having discovered that Jonathan and his armour-bearer were missing, Saul was unsure what to do. So he called for the ark of God to be brought into the camp by Ahijah the priest, one of the successors of discredited Eli – an action that had proved futile previously.

2:30-33; 4:4-11

Saul's faith, unlike his son's, was shallow. He used the ark like some lucky charm, believing its presence would ensure victory, and though he initially sought God's guidance from the priest, Saul was quick to set it aside when he saw the turmoil in the Philistines' camp increase. He felt confident he could successfully attack them.

When Saul arrived with his army he found Philistines fighting one another in the confusion, and Israelites who had joined the Philistines were now fighting against them again. Those who had been in hiding came out to fight at news that the Philistines were on the run. What is clear is that the Lord saved Israel.

The great missionary William Carey said, 'Expect great things from God; attempt great things for God.' It could well have been Jonathan's motto too! Do we expect enough from God? Are we willing to attempt the seemingly impossible should God require it?

PRAYER
Lord, you are a great God. Help me to expect great things from you and give me a willingness to attempt great things for you, whatever the obstacles.

When God is silent

So Saul asked God, 'Shall I go down and pursue the Philistines? Will you give them into Israel's hand?' But God did not answer him that day (v 37)

WHEN we pray and it seems that God is silent and not willing to answer our prayers, it is good that initially we examine ourselves and our motives. Verse 24 shows Saul's motivation to pursue the Philistines was personal revenge. They had humiliated him and rendered him impotent and unable to do anything – until Jonathan stepped in and revealed what God could do.

With this personal vendetta Saul wanted nothing less than the extermination of the Philistines, something God had not commanded. It resulted in him ordering that no man eat until evening, when battle was over, with the curse of death hanging over anyone who did. Saul's men were weary and faint with hunger. Had they been given a break and food, they would have felt refreshed and replenished – just as Jonathan was after eating the honey.

But a vengeful heart rarely pays attention to other considerations, including the needs of others. It blinded Saul to the fact that his men would have been more effective if they had been in better condition. The obedience of all Saul's men, except Jonathan, was probably out of fear of the consequences. Following the fighting they were so famished and exhausted they began slaughtering the Philistine livestock they had captured – and eating the meat with blood still in it. Saul's rash command led to his men breaking God's command.   Leviticus 17:10-12

Saul had cut short referring to God before going into battle.   v 19
Now, with his men fed and rested, he would have pursued the Philistines into the night – again without referring to God – had the priest not intervened by saying, 'Let's ask God.' When God didn't then answer his prayer, Saul would assume it was someone else's fault. He couldn't see that it might have been *him* being more concerned about avenging himself than doing what God wished, *him* ignoring the needs of his men, *him* leading them into sin.

PRAYER

Father, my passions are strong and I so easily justify myself in doing other than what you desire. When my prayers are met with silence, show me if it is due to any fault in me.

Singing in the night ... when leadership hurts

... make my joy complete by being like-minded, having the same love, being one in spirit ... In your relationships with one another, have the same mindset as Christ Jesus (vv 2, 5)

LEADERSHIP is tough! Working to unite and lead a group of unique individuals takes great wisdom, understanding, patience and love.

Paul faced a personal challenge in Philippi. We studied and reflected on that challenge in our 15 and 16 January readings. After Paul left them, was there a crisis among the believers there: differences of opinion, perhaps, concerning how he had handled that challenge? Were some arrogantly saying to the authorities, 'We follow Paul, whom you illegally imprisoned', not supporting their local church leader or arguing over in whose house they should meet?

Whatever was happening, today's passage suggests that the conflicts were caused by 'selfish ambition or vain conceit'. The problem was brought to Paul for solution.

Philippi was close to Paul's heart. We sense the pain and yearning in his words: '... *if* you have any encouragement from being united with Christ, *if* any comfort from his love, *if* any common sharing in the Spirit, *if* any tenderness and compassion ...'.

He appeals to their best selves, lifting them to a higher level, above petty arguments and self-assertion, urging them to have 'the same love, being one in spirit and of one mind', to humbly value others above themselves and to care for each other. A tall order, perhaps?

That 'each of you' phrase is interesting: is Paul reminding the troublemakers that they are included in the advice? Perhaps. And then, in verse 5 he holds up to them the example of Jesus, from which none of them could shy away.

The task of a leader is tough and lonely. Leaders can feel hurt by the behaviour and attitudes of their people. We need to love, respect and support them in prayer. Paul's advice to the Philippian Christians applies to us too. And there are words here for leaders as well: they are urged to show genuine love and care for their people, following the example of Jesus in the way they lead.

Here is a song for leaders to sing when they are hurting: 1 Kings 19:3-12 – and one for we who follow: Psalm 73:21-26. Try singing them today.

How to sing in the night

'Jesus: ... did not regard his equality with God as something he ought to exploit. Instead, he emptied himself ... he humbled himself, and became obedient ...' (vv 5-8 *BFE*)

WHAT a picture! It is not easy to take in the enormity of this description of Jesus. I feel humbled just reading it; do you? It reminds me of 2 Corinthians 8:9: 'Jesus ... though he was rich, yet for your sake he became poor, so that you through his poverty might become rich.'

After counselling the Philippians concerning 'selfish ambition' and 'vain conceit' (v 3), Paul shows them the truth about Jesus. The contrast is beyond words. I wonder how they reacted when Paul's letter was read to them. Did it lead them to repentance and renewal? Hopefully yes.

How do *you* react as you read these verses? Take a moment to reflect on them now. It may be helpful to write down your reactions and reflections. Writing can often clarify our thoughts and help us to understand more deeply.

We are on holy ground. This is the real Jesus. This is the song for us to sing at all times – and especially when we are facing challenges or tough days: when we are tempted to lose heart; to doubt the worth of following Jesus; to give up. Here is Jesus. He did all of this for us – for you, for me. Faced with the truth about Jesus, with all he went through for us, can we give up? Surely not.

But perhaps, instead of giving you hope, the picture actually discourages you. Does the great contrast between yourself and Jesus lead you to feel helpless and despairing? If so, remember why he did it; reflect on the depth of love which led him to this – his personal love for you.

Forget everyone else for a moment; see just Jesus and you. Talk to him one-to-one and allow him to comfort and reassure you. You can do this. You are not alone; you are never alone.

Whatever your own response to this picture, give yourself some time now to be with Jesus, to focus on him, to pour out your heart as you respond to him and to all that this picture says to you. He is here, he is ready.

Wise and foolish vows

'... even if the guilt lies with my son Jonathan, he must die' (v 39)

CONVINCED that someone, other than himself, had committed a sin so serious as to have God refuse to answer his prayer, Saul set about discovering who it was. Addressing his army's leaders, he told them that even if the culprit were his own son, he would be executed.

In the Bible there are several cases of people making foolish vows which, through pride and personal honour, they would not retract. For example, Jephthah vowed that if God gave him victory over the Ammonites he would sacrifice whatever came out of his house to greet him. Did he ever dream that it would be his one and only daughter? And Herod Antipas vowed that his step-daughter could have anything she wanted, up to half of his kingdom, as a reward for her dancing. Her mother advised her to ask for the head of John the Baptist on a dish. Though much distressed by the request, Herod was not prepared to retract his vow and had John beheaded.

Saul's men knew what Jonathan had done but said nothing. Their hero had risked his life to bring about God's victory and didn't deserve death for so small an offence, especially him not knowing anything of his father's command. Nevertheless, on discovering Jonathan's violation Saul was determined to fulfil his vow. His men responded with their own vow – 'Never!' With pride punctured and time wasted on this episode, Saul gave up pursuing the Philistines.

Making and keeping vows, particularly to God, is good. But we need to think carefully and prayerfully about both the promises we make and the possible consequences that might result before we make them. As a young boy aged just 15 years, William Booth vowed: 'God will have all there is of William Booth.' It was a vow he kept until his dying day, and a vow God would have us all make.

Judges 11:30-35

Mark 6:17-28

PRAYER

O Jesus, I have promised to serve thee to the end,
Be thou for ever near me, my Master and my friend.
I shall not fear the battle if thou art by my side,
Nor wander from the pathway if thou wilt be my guide.

SASB 613 v 1

(John Ernest Bode)

Pride versus humility

'... you were once small in your own eyes ...' (v 17)

THE Amalekites had been a thorn in Israel's side for centuries. Back in the wilderness they launched a cowardly attack on Israel, targeting the weary and worn-out stragglers, for which God vowed to obliterate them. They continued harassing the Israelites when they settled in Canaan, so God decided to fulfil his ancient promise by means of King Saul. *Deuteronomy 25:17-19; Exodus 17:8-16 Judges 6:3-5*

God's judgements are hard for we mere human beings to understand. But God had delayed fulfilling his vow for 400 years while the Amalekites added sin to sin. With no change in their behaviour towards God's people, and Saul failing to obey God's requirements to the full, the Amalekites continued in their cowardly conflict with Israel. It would be another 300 years before they were finally wiped out. *1 Samuel 30:1-17; 2 Samuel 1:1 1 Chronicles 4:43*

Saul's reign was one of continuing warfare. But before attacking the Amalekites, Saul compassionately let the Kenites, who lived among them, escape. Their ancestors – Reuel (also named Jethro), Moses' father-in-law and Hobab – had helped Israel in the wilderness. Even big-hearted compassion is no substitute for obedience. Other nations needed to see Israel as God's instrument of justice, not fighting for its own gain or booty. *Exodus 18; Numbers 10:29-32*

We are not told how long Saul had been king when Samuel came to him with this latest solemn message from God requiring his obedience. Only partial obedience and his erecting a monument to his own glory still revealed Saul's self-centred rebellious heart. Although in the past he didn't think himself important, that humble heart had gone forever. How often does promotion with accompanying success result in a person's proud, high and haughty view of themself.

I once read of an Eastern European leader who, when asked why an old, ragged garment was hung on his door, replied, 'It is my old shepherd's cloak and hangs there to remind me of where I came from.' May *we* ever be small in our own eyes.

PRAYER
Lord Jesus, as great as you are, you made yourself nothing. Give me a lowly view of myself. If you should give me greatness may I be forever humble.

Excuses, excuses

'But I did obey the LORD,' Saul said (v 20)

Genesis 3:11-13

WHEN we have been caught out in wrongdoing, have we noticed how quick we are to look for excuses or extenuating circumstances in an effort to vindicate ourselves? While these might be voiced, as in Adam and Eve's case, our self-justification can be something kept unexpressed in our heart.

see 14 February

Having disobeyed Samuel's instructions the first time, Saul went out to greet Samuel on his arrival. Today we find him doing the same, wishing the prophet God's blessing and boasting how he had obeyed God's command. Would Saul have needed to say that had he done so, or did he think he could fool Samuel – and indeed God? A situation not unlike that of Ananias and Sapphira.

Acts 5:1-11

Partial obedience is actually disobedience – and Samuel was having none of it! He could hear the sounds of cattle and sheep. But Saul justified himself in not killing the best livestock, claiming it was his soldiers who were responsible for bringing them back and that they were to be a sacrifice to God. Sometimes when we sin we make out that our motives were other than what they really were.

Mark 7:9-13

It is commendable to dedicate our best to God, but Jesus condemned those who declared things which might have helped their needy father or mother – 'Corban' (dedicated to God) – to avoid their responsibility towards them. God knows what lies behind the decisions we make. He wasn't fooled by Saul's claim that he had saved the animals for God.

Jeremiah 17:9

Yet Saul still would not accept God's judgement on him, claiming he *had* obeyed God. God says, 'The heart is deceitful above all things.' I would suggest the one we are most likely to deceive is ourself. Saul convinced himself that he had done nothing wrong, but God and his servant Samuel would not accept his feeble excuses.

As far as God was concerned, Saul was no longer king. Yet, although he rejected him as king, God didn't reject him as a person – for God never gives up reaching out to any of us.

PRAYER

Father, create in me a pure heart, cleanse my mind, decontaminate my motives, and make all I think, say and do a worthy offering to you.

Sad stubborn Saul

So Samuel went back with Saul, and Saul worshipped the LORD (v 31)

A TRUE penitent never shares the blame for their sin with anyone other than themself. Saul had posed as a penitent while not accepting full responsibility for his sin. He blamed his men and his fear of them. 'They made me do it', is an early claim made in childhood.

God had anointed Saul king through Samuel. Now Saul feared how losing Samuel's approval would be seen by the people. Consequently, he said what he thought Samuel wanted to hear, thinking his so-called confession and plea for Samuel's forgiveness – not God's – would persuade Samuel to again support him and go with him to worship.

When Samuel rejected his plea, Saul, in desperation tried to stop him leaving, tearing Samuel's robe in the process. In response Samuel told Saul that he was no longer Israel's king, that he had been replaced by another. Saul again pleaded for Samuel to accompany him back to worship; he did not want the elders and the rest of Israel to be aware of God's judgement on him. Appearances mattered more to Saul than the reality. He showed more concern about being honoured by the people than his own honouring of God.

Samuel conceded and went back with Saul. They arrived – and Saul worshipped the Lord. Again, I wonder what God made of such worship.

Hymnwriter John Burton (junior) pondered:

I often say my prayers; but do I ever pray?
And do the wishes of my heart go with the words I say?
For words without the heart the Lord will never hear;
Nor will he to those lips attend whose prayers are
    not sincere.   *SASB* 765 vs 1 & 3

Saul's insincerity ended his relationship with Samuel; they never saw one another again. But with a true pastor's heart, something of the heart of Jesus, Samuel mourned for him.   Luke 13:34;
                                                        19:41-44

PRAYER
Lord, help me to be honest before you, accepting even the unpalatable things you might reveal, confessing my sin with a sincere and truly repentant heart in the knowledge you love me and long to embrace me.

A king after God's own heart

'People look at the outward appearance, but the Lord looks at the heart' (v 7)

SOMETIMES it is hard to leave the past behind: it can cling to us and paralyse us, and prevent us moving on with our lives. When we experience failure, disappointment or tragedy, we can spend sleepless nights reliving, analysing and looking for ways in which things might have turned out different.

God saw something of that in dear Samuel when he ordered him to face the future and go and anoint Saul's successor. When God had Samuel anoint Saul it was in response to what the elders of Israel wanted, a king 'such as all the other nations have'. This time Samuel was directed to anoint a man who was after God's own heart.

8:5
13:14

But Samuel feared what Saul might do if he found out. (It is reassuring to know that even Samuel's faith was mixed with a modicum of doubt.) He knew Saul well. There's no telling what a person with an inflated ego might be prepared to do when offended. But God had Samuel's fear covered and, whatever fear remained, Samuel obeyed.

On meeting seven of Jesse's sons Samuel saw three very likely candidates – men's men who were part of King Saul's army, but neither they nor the other four were God's choice. The youngest son, David, out tending sheep, was disregarded as a likely candidate by his father.

17:13

This reminds me of Gladys Aylward, who was so slow learning the language that the China Inland Mission decided to reject her application to be a missionary there. But God had other ideas. God can see what people are often blind to – the heart and the potential of someone totally surrendered to him.

Saul had been unwilling to surrender himself to God's sovereignty. Though no longer king in God's eyes, he continued to sit on the throne and act as though he was. Then David came on the scene as a blessing and a saviour to Saul. At no point did David ever attempt to take by force the throne that was rightfully his. Neither does our Saviour Jesus. We have to vacate it and offer him his rightful place.

PRAYER
Lord Jesus, I vacate my throne and surrender the sovereignty of my life to you. By right it is yours, my Saviour, God and King.

Singing in the night ... a song of testimony

He reached down from on high and took hold of me; he drew me out of deep waters (v 16)

FOR dramatic effect, Psalm 18 equals any science fiction film! Imagine the drama unfolding as you read. Sense the panic and fear in verses 4-6; the unleashing of power as God expresses his anger in verses 7-15; his majesty as 'he soared on the wings of the wind' and as 'with hailstones and bolts of lightning' he 'thundered from heaven ... and scattered the enemy'! It is the kind of fantastic action which might send some of us to hide behind the sofa if it were a film!

And then feel the enormous contrast expressed in verse 16; the gentleness and love of God for his follower. This is surely the most amazing rescue mission.

In panic, fear and distress, the writer called to God. God answered beyond his wildest dreams. So, is this a psalm about answered prayer? Well, yes, it is. In seeking him, we open ourselves for him to act in us and for us. That allows him to work much more effectively.

God is *always* more than willing to act on our behalf, but without our consent and invitation he cannot do all that he wishes to do.

A 'spacious place' (v 19) is a safe place, where the enemy can be spotted from far away and cannot creep up unseen. When we say 'yes' to God, he brings us to that place, which Psalm 91:1, 3-4 – using different pictures – calls his 'shadow' and 'under his wings'.

God was angry because his follower was under attack. He used the powers at his disposal to deal thoroughly with the attackers. He is ready to do the same for us: to bring us also into a safe place, under his protection. It may not be as dramatic as in Psalm 18 but it will be just as safe and secure.

Perhaps the song of verses 1-19 is also your testimony. If so, sing it to God and to others. And we all can sing verses 28-36, to lift our own spirits. Reflecting on God's faithfulness in the past encourages the present. Try it today.

Singing in the night ... in the face of tragedy

Though the fig-tree does not bud and there are no grapes on the vines,... though there are no sheep in the sheepfold and no cattle in the stalls, yet ... I will be joyful in God my Saviour (vv 17-18)

IF you have never read Habakkuk before, you are in good company! It is certainly a lesser-known Old Testament book. Prophet Habakkuk speaks of God's action to save his people, whose very existence was being threatened by enemies – rather like in Psalm 18, which we read yesterday.

Earlier in the book Habakkuk questions the bad things which were happening. God promises that he is in control of the terrifying events. Then in today's reading Habakkuk expresses acceptance and commitment.

When bad things happen, we easily question God or assume that he is acting in anger or vengeance. God is happy to be questioned. He can readily absorb all our anger, hurt and bewilderment. And when we have finished shouting, he is eager to show us the truth and calm our fears.

The truth is that God is love; mercy; grace. He will never cause suffering, even though Old Testament writers, with limited early understanding of God, sometimes suggest otherwise. The Word of God is whole, complete, Old and New Testaments together, and the unified picture it gives is that, like a good father, God may allow hurtful experiences to happen to us, knowing that we can grow through them – but will never deliberately cause them.

Habakkuk's response demonstrates his trust in God's care. God weeps when his children suffer; stands alongside them; provides for them through the care of others and the discoveries of science. He is not darkness, destruction or vengeance; he is love and light, life and grace, goodness and truth (see 1 John 1:5; 3:1; 4:7-10).

We have seen so much goodness in the past two years. God has used the terrible experience of the pandemic, in which he has wept with us, to inspire practical love and grace. If you are still living through the dark results of this experience, God is in it with you. He will never abandon you.

Like the surefootedness of deer, Habakkuk's song in verses 17-19 ends with confidence in God. God can lead us to 'the heights' of his love and grace – and strengthen our confidence in him, too. Take time to reflect on this and make Habakkuk's song your own.

An unlikely disciple

Meanwhile, Saul was still breathing out murderous threats against the Lord's disciples (v 1)

SAUL – later named Paul, so let's continue with his new name – was of the tribe of Benjamin. No one had a better pedigree than Paul: circumcised on the eighth day following his birth, an Israelite, a Hebrew of Hebrews; with regards to the religious law, a Pharisee; as for zeal, he persecuted the fledgling church; as for righteousness based on the law, he was faultless. *Philippians 3:5-6*

But though Paul was thoroughly trained in the law by someone acknowledged as one of the nation's greatest teachers, Gamaliel, he lacked Gamaliel's grace and tolerance. *Acts 22:3* For it was Gamaliel's intervention that prevented the Sanhedrin lynching Peter and the other disciples. *5:33-40*

Paul was the leading activist in attempting to destroy the church, going from house to house, dragging off both men and women to prison. He hunted them down in foreign cities, *8:3* trying to make them blaspheme, and was complicit in their murders. Yet God had his eye on Paul, along with a plan for *22:4; 26:10-11* him. The Lord also had a shock in store for him as he made his way to Damascus – a shock that would change his life forever.

By striking him down and leaving him in darkness for three days, God surely brought to Paul's attention how spiritually blind he was. Not an easy thing for such a proud Pharisee to accept! We too can be sincere, enthusiastic for God, *see John ch 9:39-41* adamant that our views and actions are in accord with his will, dismissing those of others, and yet be wrong. It always requires a miracle for God's light to pierce such blindness.

Selecting Paul, God chose someone most unlikely – as he frequently does even today. I've seen God miraculously transform people from being aggressively opposed to him and become ardent witnesses of the gospel. No wonder William Booth, Founder of The Salvation Army, challenged his troops: 'Go for souls, and go for the worst.'

PRAYER
Lord, help me to see others through your eyes and to have faith in what you can do for and through the most unlikely people.

ACTS 9:10-19

A courageous disciple

'Brother Saul, the Lord – Jesus, who appeared to you on the road as you were coming here – has sent me...' (v 17)

24:14

HAVE you ever sensed the Lord telling you to do something you have been frightened to do, maybe something which seemed utter foolishness? That was Ananias's experience. Paul's fanatical reputation spread far and wide. When followers of 'the Way' knew he was heading in their direction, they feared what was in store for them. Consequently, when Ananias had his vision he could hardly believe what he was being told to do.

Meanwhile Paul, awakened to the wickedness of what he had been doing, was praying. Conviction of sin will always drive us to prayer. The worse our sin, the worse we feel. Paul had been unable to eat or drink, and probably sleep. God told Ananias what had happened to Paul, adding that Paul was expecting him to come and lay hands on him and restore his sight, both physically and spiritually no doubt. But Ananias was apprehensive; he knew what a terrible man Paul was.

Again God ordered Ananias, 'Go!' Sometimes preachers speak of God asking or requesting something of us. God doesn't ask or request. He is God, King of kings and Lord of lords. He orders, he commands and we either obey or disobey. On ordering Ananias a second time, the Lord added a little of what he had in mind for Paul. In response, whatever his fears, Ananias obeyed.

Paul must have been deeply touched on hearing Ananias's tender words, 'Brother Saul.' He, whom Paul would have wished dead only a few days ago, was embracing him with the love of a brother. Humbly, this previously proud Pharisee accepted the laying on of the very hands he had sought to bind – and the Holy Spirit filled him.

We hear nothing more of Ananias. In itself the task was a small albeit scary one, but the consequences were enormous. Ananias may have never known the importance of what he did that day.

PRAYER
Lord Jesus, give me the courage and willingness to do what you desire even if it scares me. Remind me that the consequences of even a seemingly small task may be greater than I could ever imagine.

An encouraging disciple

But Barnabas took him and brought him to the apostles (v 27)

HAVE you ever had a nickname? When I was a child most of my friends only knew me by my nickname. At nearly 40 years of age and living miles from where I grew up, I had not heard the name for years. Then, one winter's night there was a knock at our front door and I opened it. A couple stood there, who I didn't recognise in the dark.

'Hello, Froggy,' they both said. Immediately I knew they were from my past. Passing through the city, these old friends decided to surprise my wife and I. Why Froggy? I've no idea. Some nicknames are descriptive or complimentary; others quite hurtful and damaging.

Jesus gave some disciples nicknames. He called James and John 'Boanerges', meaning 'Sons of Thunder', probably because of their hot-headed aggressive natures. For instance, they wanted to call fire down on a Samaritan village that rejected Jesus on his way to Jerusalem. However, Jesus only referred to them by that name once. Was it because God would change their natures, for James became the first apostle to be martyred and John eventually became known as the apostle of love.

Mark 3:17

Luke 9:51-56

Conversely, the nickname Jesus gave Simon described what he was yet to be rather than what he was. He would waver when he walked on the water and later deny he even knew Jesus, yet Jesus gave him the name Peter, 'The Rock' – something he definitely was not, but something he one day would become.

John 1:42;
Matthew 16:18

The nickname Barnabas, or 'Son of Encouragement', was given Joseph by the apostles who recognised him to be an exceptional encourager. His sacrificial giving encouraged the church. He believed in Paul and the validity of his story when no one else did, and was prepared to put his reputation on the line in backing him. Nor was he prepared to give up on John Mark when he let him and Paul down.

Acts 4:36-37

13:13; 15:36-41

What nickname would you like to be known by? In being called Christian we carry the name above all names.

PRAYER

Jesus, we carry your great name in the label 'Christian'. Make us worthy of it, Lord.

A giving disciple

All the widows stood round him, crying and showing him the robes and other clothing that Dorcas had made while she was still with them (v 39)

Acts 10:38

JESUS 'went around doing good'. Tabitha – or Dorcas, as we usually refer to her – may not have travelled around but she certainly did much good just where she was. 'Love your neighbour as yourself', was a command of Jesus to his disciples. Again, Dorcas's love for her neighbours was evident to Peter as the widows, weeping together in her room, showed him the garments Dorcas had made for them.

Mark 12:31

Some people are very good with words but fall short when it comes to works. The validity of our faith is seen in what we do. The widows revealed the fruit of Dorcas's faith. She wasn't someone who merely wished the poor and needy well; she did something about it. Possibly not rich enough to purchase the garments people needed, she made them. Generosity and self-sacrifice are not confined to the finances we have. Our time and labour can be equally costly.

James 2:14-26

2 Corinthians 9:8-11

God always gives us sufficient means to be generous. True generosity is a thing of the heart. When collecting for a good cause, often I've had people give nothing at all yet promise to make a generous donation should they win the lottery. Dorcas didn't wait with the intention of giving from hoped-for riches, she gave of what she had. Hers was a life of always giving, of sacrificial love towards her neighbours. She was a light in the lives of those around her – just as Jesus had taught – and when she died it was as if that light had gone out.

Matthew 5:16

Dorcas may not have been good with words but she offered what she had to God, her needlework skills, and glorified God with them. All that we do, even the most menial task, when given as an offering to please him is worship. Nor should we compare our offering with that which others give. We cannot see their hearts. Jesus values even the smallest thing given with the right heart.

Luke 21:1-4

PRAYER

Lord Jesus, give me a heart like Dorcas, a heart like yours, always giving to others.

A healing disciple

Peter sent them out of the room; then he got down on his knees and prayed (v 40)

IN Acts we see the remarkable transformation of a fisherman
– 'unschooled', very 'ordinary' – into an extraordinary leader,   4:13
preacher and healer. The gospel net he cast with his sermon
on the day of Pentecost resulted in an astonishing catch of
3,000 souls. It must surely have reminded him of what Christ   2:41
predicted following the amazing catch of fish he had in
response to obeying Jesus when first they met, as well as the   Luke 5:1-11
Lord's unbelievable promise that his followers would do even
greater things than they had seen him do!   John 14:12
    The church was now scattered beyond Jerusalem and   8:4
Peter, with a heart for the Lord's people, travelled about the
country visiting them. Arriving at Lydda and finding Aeneas,
a man paralysed and bedridden for eight years, Peter boldly
declared, 'Jesus Christ heals you' – in other words, 'You *are*
healed Aeneas. Get up and roll up your mat, you won't be
needing it anymore.' Though guided by the Holy Spirit, was
Peter also remembering what he learnt from Jesus when he
healed paralysed people?   Mark 2:10-11;
    When Peter received the call to go to Dorcas, did it remind   John 5:8,11
him of when he witnessed Jesus restore Jairus's dead daughter
to life? Peter was one of only three disciples who saw what
Jesus did that day. Having sent all the mourners out of the
room, Jesus took the little girl's hand and told her, 'Get up.'   Mark 5:37-42
Peter too sent all the mourners out of the room. Having first
prayed, he told Dorcas, 'Get up' – and like Jesus he took Dorcas
by *her* hand, helping her to her feet.
    I am reminded of the wristbands which were prevalent
some years ago. They had the letters WWJD, standing for
'What Would Jesus Do?' I'm sure Peter wasn't attempting to
copy precisely what he witnessed, but wanted to approach the
situation in the same way as Jesus would have done. May that
be our desire and prayer in every situation we meet.

PRAYER
Lord Jesus, guide me in all I think, say and do, and send your
Spirit to give me power and boldness.

Singing in the night ... a song of victory (1)

'The Lᴏʀᴅ is my strength and my defence; he has become my salvation. He is my God, and I will praise him' (v 2)

THE great escape! God enabled Moses and the Israelites to leave Egypt at the shortest notice, to avoid the wrath of Pharaoh (see Exodus 11 and 12:29-42). When they had safely crossed the sea to the east of Egypt and the Egyptian army had sunk beneath the waves, they sang in praise of God. Miriam echoed the song, tambourine in hand (vv 20-21).

How did they manage to compose such a song at short notice, exhausted as they must have been after hours of great stress? We cannot know. Perhaps we can ask Moses when we reach Heaven; that would be an interesting conversation!

The song recounts the event in detail: '"Pharaoh's chariots and his army he has hurled into the sea"' (v 4); '"your burning anger ... consumed them like stubble. By the blast of your nostrils the waters piled up"' (vv 7-8). *The Message* paraphrase is even more dramatic: 'Gᴏᴅ ... *pitched* horse and rider into the sea'; 'Pharoah's chariots and army he *dumped* in the sea'; 'Your strong right hand, Gᴏᴅ ... *shatters* the enemy' (vv 1, 4, 6) [my italics].

Feel their euphoria as, in the release of tension, they relive what has happened and realise that God has rescued them. Some verses are like Psalm 18, which we considered in last Saturday's reading. Such parallels often appear in Old Testament writings: a pattern of praise, lifting God high.

To retell the story *after* the event is very therapeutic. It helps us to process the fear and anxiety – and eventually to move forward. They needed so much to do this – and so do we at times.

What are your first thoughts after great stress and anxiety, when you realise that at last all is well? The Israelites would have counted heads first, to make sure no one had been lost – and we would do the same – but then came the song. When palpable relief sets in, our relationship with Jesus naturally leads us to thank him. No other words are necessary; he knows our gratitude and our trust in him.

Maybe this is a good day to sing this song for yourself – adjusting the words to fit your own situation.

Singing in the night … a song of victory (2)

'In your unfailing love you will lead the people you have redeemed. In your strength you will guide them to your holy dwelling' (v 13)

YESTERDAY we reflected on the Israelites' first reactions after crossing the sea safely. Now their song continues, moving beyond the actual events, to focus on God himself rather than on what God does. It goes more deeply, speaking of God's unfailing love and how he guides them to his holy place.

They are glorying in God's power and authority – and in the fact that he is *their* God, always there for them, to fight for them in every circumstance. Taking no glory for themselves, they attribute to God all aspects of the victory. They could have praised Moses' leadership – for he did get them out of Egypt and shepherd them over the sea. They could have praised each other, saying, 'Didn't we do well to get over safely before the waves returned!' But no; all the praise was for God alone.

The song looks more widely too, placing God above the gods of other nations around. And when the surrounding nations heard of what God had done, they would allow the Israelites to travel unchallenged towards the land God had prepared for them (vv 15-17) and to settle there in peace. That would prove how great God is.

Such deeper praise requires us first to slow down, to breathe more deeply, to reflect on what has happened. Perhaps there are two kinds of praise, then: the instant reaction we saw yesterday – and the deeper reflection which realises God's greatness and recognises our own relationship with him.

Praising God in daily life can lead to daily victory: 'So shall each fear, each fret, each care be turned into a song' (*SASB* 361). This is a good place to begin.

> Fill thou my life, O Lord my God, in every part with praise,
> That my whole being may proclaim thy being and thy ways.
> Not for the lip of praise alone, nor e'en the praising heart
> I ask, but for a life made up of praise in every part! (v 1)
>
> So shall no part of day or night from sacredness be free;
> But all my life, in every step, be fellowship with thee. (v 4)
>
> (Horatius Bonar)

The God-fearing centurion

He and all his family were devout and God-fearing; he gave generously to those in need and prayed to God regularly (v 2)

CENTURIONS were the backbone of the Roman army, in command of one hundred men. Polybius, a Greek historian, wrote: 'Centurions are required not to be bold and adventurous so much as good leaders, of steady and prudent mind ... able when overwhelmed and hard-pressed to stand fast and die at their post.'

Luke 7:1-10

Mark 15:39

Acts 27:1, 3; 42-43

A number of centurions appear in the New Testament. The first Gentile to seek Jesus' help was a centurion; the first Gentile to witness that Jesus was the Son of God was a centurion; a kind centurion named Julius was responsible for safely delivering Paul to Rome, saving his life in the process.

Cornelius was stationed in Caesarea, Rome's regional headquarters. Reaching out from the confines of his own upbringing and culture, and the unsatisfactory Roman religion with its belief in multifarious gods, he was drawn towards the truths within Jewish religion. The term 'God-fearing Gentile' refers to an adherent, someone who attended the synagogue without the full commitment of a circumcised proselyte. Such was Cornelius and all his family.

I would love to know the influences and course of events that led to Cornelius, his family and the soldier mentioned becoming devout and God-fearing. Cornelius was sincere in his openness to God and regular prayer, and had a compassion and generosity towards others. It was while praying that the angel of God appeared to Cornelius.

v 30

When we seek God we often discover a previously hidden vapour trail in our past experiences that reveals how God had been always seeking us. God was undoubtedly seeking Cornelius and accepted the alms and prayers he offered in his pursuit of God.

There are many people like Cornelius today – spiritual, believing in God, generous, praying people who are not committed to any particular religious group. Though not far from the Kingdom, they have yet to know Jesus and be part of God's family. How are they to find what is missing?

see Romans
10:11-15

PRAYER

Cornelius was not far from your Kingdom, Lord. Show me how to share the truth about you with similar people I know who are not yet committed to you.

The beginning of Peter's learning curve

'Do not call anything impure that God has made clean' (v 15)

PETER grew up complying with the strict Jewish dietary law which prohibited eating certain foods considered unclean. Although Jesus' disciples may have paid little attention to man-made rules such as ritual hand-washing, God's law was a very different matter. How often has religion degenerated into rule-keeping and outward observances rather than how a person's heart is towards both God and other people.

Leviticus 11

Mark 7:1-5

Mark 12:30-31

At prayer on the roof of Simon the tanner's house, Peter became very hungry and fell into a trance as he became totally focused on God. Such prayer is like building a staircase to Heaven down which God is able to descend and make his presence felt. It isn't easy to pray like that. Though I might shut the door of my prayer room, shutting the door of my mind to the noise of intrusive thoughts is quite another thing.

With Peter's stomach crying out for food, God revealed a sheet descending from the sky. It was filled with every kind of creature. 'Kill and eat,' commanded God. No way was Peter going to do that. Although it is commendable not to allow one's stomach to overrule one's principles, Peter was defying the command of the One who made the law and can alter it if he so pleases.

Philippians 3:19

God rebuked Peter and repeated his command – something he needs to do with us on occasions. Then, as Peter wondered what it all meant, the Gentile messengers Cornelius had sent arrived and God told Peter he was to go wherever they wanted to take him. Peter not only went down to meet his visitors but also invited them to stay overnight. He would never have done this before.

v 28

Jesus promised his disciples that the Holy Spirit would both teach and remind his followers of things he said. Did the Holy Spirit bring to Peter's remembrance what Jesus said about unclean food, and what was the Holy Spirit teaching him in relation to other things Jesus said?

John 14:26

Mark 7:14-19

Matthew 28:19; Acts 1:8

PRAYER

Father, help me not to be so locked in my views of right and wrong that I fail to hear what you may be saying to me.

God has no favourites

'I now realise how true it is that God does not show favouritism but accepts from every nation the one who fears him and does what is right' (vv 34-35)

CORNELIUS surely warned his messengers to be sensitive and courteous to Jewish feelings, for on reaching Simon the tanner's house they 'stopped at the gate'. But (as we read yesterday) by inviting them to join him as overnight guests Peter broke with Jewish convention – as he later did by entering Cornelius's house.

v 17

God prepared Cornelius and Peter independently in readiness for meeting each other. He did the same with Paul and Ananias, and it's something he still does today.

Acts 9:11-12

Sometimes we can feel compelled to do a thing, like visit someone or make a phone call, yet not know why – only to discover the plan God has in place when we do it. Peter had no idea why he had been sent until Cornelius described what happened to him three days earlier, adding that his close friends and relatives had come together so they too could hear all God wanted Peter to say.

While Peter was speaking, the Holy Spirit suddenly came down upon everyone gathered there, just as he did upon the Jewish disciples gathered in the upper room at Pentecost.

Peter's astonished Jewish companions were left in no doubt that God has no favourites, that Jew and Gentile are equally precious and loved by God. Consequently, Peter saw no reason why they could not all be baptised. How could they be refused the symbol having received the reality it signifies?

No doubt hungry to know more, they had Peter stay with them a few days, for this was not the end of their search but the beginning of their new life with much to learn.

Although the message here is clear, sadly churches have not always lived up to it. They haven't readily accepted people of different race, culture or social class as equals. In many congregations they can still be made to feel outsiders, like the Gentiles of Jesus' day who were confined to the periphery of the Temple.

PRAYER

Heavenly Father, send your light-revealing Holy Spirit to expose and take down the barriers in your Church – and open my eyes to any blindness I have to the very same barriers in me.

Criticised for doing the right thing

So when Peter went up to Jerusalem, the circumcised believers criticised him (v 2)

NEWS of Peter fraternising with Gentiles spread throughout the Church and many circumcised believers in Jerusalem were offended by what they heard. The Church had experienced peace following Paul's conversion. Such action by a high-profile Jew like   28 February
Peter could well have got the Church a bad name among Jews outside the Church and stirred up a new episode of hostility.

Often the Church has been more concerned about its own reputation than doing the right thing and being condemned for it. That can be true of individual Christians too. Are we sometimes more concerned by what others might think or how things might appear, rather than doing what God would have us do? Jesus was often misjudged and severely criticised for what he did, but he did what was right whatever the consequences. It particularly hurts when criticism comes from   Luke 15:1-2, 19:7;
brothers and sisters in Christ.   Matthew 9:10-11

In the late 1700s, a young minister questioned why the Church didn't make more effort to share the good news in foreign lands. An elderly minster purportedly got up and said, 'Young man, sit down! You are an enthusiast. When God wants to convert the heathen, he will do it without consulting you or me.' Despite such discouraging criticism, William Carey later pioneered the vision God gave him and became a missionary to India, inspiring missionary endeavour in others.

In response to his critics, Peter described what happened in detail, making clear that it was Holy Spirit instigated and orchestrated. Hearing how the Holy Spirit descended in power as he had at Pentecost, with the Gentiles experiencing all that the Jewish believers had experienced, put the matter beyond doubt. God had given the Gentiles the same gift he gave the Jews.

Peter never defended himself. He merely let the facts, which his six companions could verify, speak for themselves. So his listeners conceded and rejoiced at discovering, like Peter, that the gate to the Kingdom of God was wider than they had realised.

PRAYER
Father, help me to respond to unjust criticism with grace, and not let it stop me from doing what you desire – whatever the consequences.

God at work

The Lord's hand was with them, and a great number of people believed and turned to the Lord (v 21)

SOMETIMES circumstances force us to do what we should have been doing in the first place. In an effort to destroy the Early Church, Satan actually helped it to fulfil Christ's mandate for it. The believers escaping persecution fled Jerusalem and were scattered far and wide. But they took God's message of salvation with them, sharing the good news of Jesus with fellow Jews wherever they found themselves.

Matthew 28:19-20

Acts 8:4

Luke focuses on Philip because he 'proclaimed the Messiah' to the half-Jewish Samaritans, who believed in the coming Messiah. Hearing that Samaritans were accepting Philip's message, the church in Jerusalem sent Peter and John to check it out. Having witnessed the authenticity of what God was doing there, they preached in Samaritan villages themselves as they returned to Jerusalem.

v 5

v 14

v 25

But still the message wasn't being proclaimed to Gentiles. Even when Peter shared with Cornelius's non-Jewish guests it was not something initiated by Peter, nor a planned mission to reach Gentiles. However, in Antioch ordinary believers were now telling the Greeks the gospel and they were responding as God blessed their ministry.

When news of this reached the Jerusalem church, the representative they sent this time was Barnabas – a man 'full of the Holy Spirit and faith'. He was so pleased with what he found there and encouraged everyone in their new-found faith. He was also wise and humble enough to know he required the help of someone more capable than himself to do what needed to be done, and he knew Paul was the man.

What a remarkable character Barnabas was; what pains he took to draw Paul towards the mission God had planned for him. Barnabas surely knew that outstandingly-gifted Paul would one day outshine him. May we too be as willing to lift someone when it might mean a lower position for ourselves – just as John the Baptist had done with Jesus.

John 3:30

PRAYER

Lord Jesus, grant me a heart willing to give way to others better than myself. Destroy any personal ambition so that I always put your Kingdom and your glory at the centre of my living.

Singing in the night ... a song of hope

Strengthen the feeble hands, steady the knees that give way; say to those with fearful hearts, 'Be strong, do not fear; your God will come ... to save you' (vv 3-4)

SPRINGTIME will soon arrive in the northern hemisphere. Flowers will appear; birds will sing; the earth will awaken after winter. It may have already begun! Isaiah pictures it beautifully: 'The wilderness ... will burst into bloom ... The glory of Lebanon ... Carmel and Sharon ... will see ... the splendour of our God.' Lebanon, where mighty cedar trees grew; Carmel the 'garden-land';[8] Sharon with rich soil, covered with wild flowers[9] – all will burst into life again.

God's people had split into two separate nations, their leaders focusing on their own power instead of God's. Both were threatened by surrounding nations – and by each other! Through years of unrest and turmoil the people had become discouraged, feeble-handed, weak. It was like winter (see Isaiah 33:7-9).

But now Isaiah brings hope. They are still God's people; God is still acting on their behalf; their future will be brighter.

Under prolonged difficulty and challenge, weighed down by cares and concerns, we all tend to become stooped, looking downwards and inwards, blind to the good things around us; deaf to words of hope. Our world view shrinks. It is a normal reaction. Isaiah urges the people of Judah to stop looking down – like people with weak knees walking on rough ground – and to look up, take courage, find new hope: 'Be strong, don't be afraid, there is your God. ... he will come and deliver you' (v 4 *BFE*).

Just as the world seems to yawn and stretch in springtime, awakening to new life and wonder, so will our spirits when we look up to God. He will give new hope, new vision, new purpose. The promise could not be clearer. God has this in his control.

The materials of springtime have not changed: the soil, birds and trees are the same, but life stirs within them, making them fresh and new. When we look up to God, our circumstances might not change, but our attitudes towards them will. We will awaken to new possibilities, new growth in ourselves, new strength and determination to face the challenges with God.

Today's reading is one to pray and sing whenever we need new hope. Try it just now.

Singing in the night ... a song of joy

... those the LORD has rescued will return. They will enter Zion with singing; ... Gladness and joy will overtake them, and sorrow and sighing will flee away (v 10)

SPRINGTIME needs water – and it was promised in abundance: 'Water will gush forth in the wilderness ... The burning sand will become a pool, the thirsty ground bubbling springs' (vv 6-7). If you have ever lived or travelled in desert areas you will know how amazing this promise is. In a semi-desert area I once tried to shelter under a cactus tree – the only vegetation in sight – when our vehicle became stuck in the dry sand. Water was on everyone's mind.

The hope which we reflected upon yesterday grew into joy as God's hand was seen in the lives and world of his people. Isaiah writes as though the water itself were dancing for joy, as indeed it might, for this would be a time of refreshment and healing for Judah: spiritually, emotionally, even physically. Weak ones would become strong; deficiencies and failings would be dealt with and replaced by health and growth; life would burst forth in the desert land.

But a flurry of new life was only the beginning. God wanted his people to move into the future with confidence and joy; so, he would open a new 'highway' where formerly feeble legs could walk safely. Even more, it would be a 'Way of Holiness', free from terrors and dangers, where they could travel through life within his care. Contrast this again with 33:8-9.

God's way is a safe place, protected by his love and grace. Psalm 91:4 gives the same assurance differently, picturing a mother hen protecting her chicks: 'He will cover you with his feathers, and under his wings you will find refuge.' What a cause for 'everlasting joy'!

The promise remains true. God wants to bring refreshment of spirit, mind and body – new life! And when we have been revived and refreshed, he leads us into his own pathway, where he will be present always to help us over rough places, so that we walk with confidence in him each day.

Are you needing that revival, that promise, that infusion of hope and joy – or even just a reassuring reminder that you are already on his highway? Then sing Isaiah's song today.

A not so obvious miracle

The disciples, as each one was able, decided to provide help for the brothers and sisters living in Judea (v 29)

JOHN STOTT, an Anglican theologian, wrote: 'It is difficult for us to grasp the impassable gulf which yawned between the Jews on the one hand and the Gentiles (including even the "God-fearers") on the other.'[10] Israel became aware of being different to other nations, dedicated and separated to God, following the Exodus and the covenant at Mount Sinai. Throughout its history, the temptation to compromise with the idolatry and immorality of nearby nations plagued Israel.

Exodus 19:5-6

Following the Exile, the Jews returned to an even bigger danger – the corruptness and compromise among their fellow Jews who had remained in Canaan. The continuing threat of contamination led to a hardened and superior attitude towards other nations, and the false assumption that they were special to God to the exclusion of others. This blinded them to God's great plan for the nation, that of revealing God's salvation to the world – something eventually fulfilled by Jesus.

Ezra 9:1-2

Isaiah 42:6; 49:6
John 8:12

Tacitus, the Roman historian, stated that Jews 'regard the rest of mankind with all the hatred of enemies.' In that context, what those Gentile disciples at Antioch did for the Jewish believers in Jerusalem, many who at one time would have hated Gentiles, is an amazing, generous gesture – a miracle, no less.

A new convert, so grateful to God for all he had done for him in bringing him to Jesus and transforming his life, placed a wad of notes in the offering plate as it was passed among the congregation. (He had not yet been given envelopes in which to place his offering.) Although he attempted to do this discretely, the church member sitting next to him was watching and commented, 'You really don't need to give that much!'

Giving is always an expression of love and gratitude. One cannot love and not give. Giving is also a hallmark of faith. Those who received what Barnabas and Paul brought must have been deeply moved by what those Gentiles did and convinced of what God had done in their hearts too.

Luke 7:36-47

PRAYER
Lord Jesus, you have done so much for me; in love and deep gratitude I give my all to you.

God can do the impossible

So Peter was kept in prison, but the church was earnestly praying to God for him (v 5)

THE King Herod in our passage was Agrippa the First, son of Aristobulus who had been executed by his paranoid father, Herod the Great. Agrippa grew up and was educated in Rome. When his friend Caligula became emperor, Agrippa received the title 'king' and a domain in Israel. Arriving in Jerusalem from Rome, Agrippa cultivated the popularity of the people with his strict observance of Jewish religious practices and the Law.

We don't know why he then began arresting members, probably leaders, of the church. Maybe news of the church's acceptance of Gentiles had reached his ears and offended his religious sensibilities. We are also not told what James was charged with or anything of his trial, just that his execution pleased the Jews – and so this resulted in Herod arresting Peter. We recall how James and his brother John once sought a 'crown' from Christ. In response, Jesus promised them a cup; they would share his cup of suffering.

Mark 10:35-39

Peter was arrested and was placed under maximum security, ensuring that he could not escape or be rescued – perhaps a reminder to Peter of a previous instance? Herod was obliged to delay his planned prosecution of Peter as no trial or execution could take place during the seven days' Festival of Unleavened Bread. We are not told how many days Peter was incarcerated. Bound with chains to a soldier either side of him, with others on guard by the door, Peter couldn't possibly escape.

Matthew 27:65-66

But we have a God who can do the impossible, and Peter had friends who knew how to pray! They were praying unceasingly, earnestly banging on Heaven's door. How often does a church gather together and pray like that? Yet God promises, 'Call to Me, and I will answer you, and show you great and mighty things, which you do not know.'

Jeremiah 33:3
NKJV

PRAYER

Forgive us for our lack of prayer,
When you commanded, 'Come to me,'
We made excuses, disobeyed
And in our blindness failed to see
Things great and mighty set aside,
For those who pray, God will provide.   (H.W.)

Breaking the chains

He [an angel] struck Peter on the side and woke him up. 'Quick, get up!' he said, and the chains fell off Peter's wrists (v 7)

IN Hebrews 12:1, Paul encourages us to 'throw off everything that hinders *and* the sin that so easily entangles'. It's not just sin that is our problem. Satan will use things that in themselves are quite innocent and harmless to alter our priorities and divert our attention and energies from what God desires.

When it comes to sin, we can so easily sleepwalk into it. We may not intend to paddle in its waters at all, never mind wade in deeper, but why is it we sometimes foolishly go down to the beach and stand near the water's edge in the first place? Eve's foolishness was that she did not keep well away from the tree that bore forbidden fruit. She may not have intended eating from it, but as she stood there looking at the fruit, so attractive and seemingly beneficial, everything God had said went out of the window.

Genesis 3:6

Sin so readily entangles its victim as securely as Peter's chains had hold of him. Society may be quick to judge drug addicts and alcoholics, but we all have sinful tendencies of one kind or another, even if invisible to anyone else. It might be gossiping, speaking ill of others, lying to get ourselves out of a difficult situation, a jealous or envious trait. These can easily become addictions we find impossible to break, whereby Satan holds us in his grip.

But our God can do the impossible. Those chains that so tightly bind us, he alone can break. How wonderful it is to have persistent praying friends like Peter had! For some of us, it was through the unceasing prayers of godly friends or family that our chains fell off and we were set free.

v 5

> Long my imprisoned spirit lay
> Fast bound in sin and nature's night;
> Thine eye diffused a quickening ray;
> I woke; the dungeon flamed with light.
> My chains fell off, my heart was free,
> I rose, went forth, and followed thee.   (Charles Wesley)

SASB 241 v 3

PRAYER

Thank you, Father, for friends and family who faithfully prayed for my salvation; also for answering their prayers and setting me free.

Unexpected answer to prayer

But Peter kept on knocking, and when they opened the door and saw him, they were astonished (v 16)

Acts 6:8–7:60

ONE wonders why Luke says nothing regarding James's trial, yet records what happened to Stephen so fully and here records Peter's escape from Herod's clutches in detail too. Why, too, did God not save James as he did Peter? While the Bible reveals so much about God, much remains a mystery.

To Peter it all seemed like a dream – being woken by an angel with his chains just falling off, walking past guards unchallenged, the main prison gate opening by itself. Not until he was out on the street did he realise what he thought was a vision was actually real.

The believers were gathered in prayer in a house stated to be that of Mary, rather than her husband. This would indicate she was a widow – and a wealthy one at that, since the house was big enough to accommodate 'many people', and she had at least one servant too. Peter knew exactly where to find his friends.

When Peter knocked on the door, those inside were unaware that their prayers had already been answered. Having possibly prayed for days, they knew Peter's planned trial and anticipated execution were now only hours away. Sometimes God allows things to go to the extreme before he reveals his answer, and he often does not give what he desires to give until he sees we want it enough. Jesus taught us to be persistent in our petitions.

Luke 11:5-10; 18:1-8

What were the believers expecting God to do as they prayed: that Peter would be found innocent and freed? God's answers are frequently far greater than our prayers. They definitely did not expect God to do what he did! They didn't believe Rhoda, despite her insisting that Peter was outside, and were astonished to see Peter standing there when they eventually opened the door.

'Whenever I have prayed earnestly, I have been heard and have obtained more than I prayed for,' said Martin Luther. 'God sometimes delays, but he always comes.'

PRAYER

Ephesians 3:20

Father, give me a faith in the power of prayer, believing that you are 'able to do immeasurably more than all I ask or imagine'.

God's justice

Immediately, because Herod did not give praise to God, an angel of the Lord struck him down, and he was eaten by worms and died (v 23)

ARE you troubled by the question, 'Why do good and godly people so often suffer while the wicked prosper?' So were many a Bible writer, such as Jeremiah and Job.

In Psalm 73, while Asaph accepted that God is good to the pure in heart, he went on to say how he nearly lost his spiritual footing through envying the arrogant with their prosperity and easy life. It made his efforts to be pure and righteous seem pointless, until he considered the bigger picture of the transient nature of this present life, and the incomparable blessing of being close to God.

Although the Bible clearly points to the ultimate punishment of the wicked beyond this life, occasionally God administered punishment in the present – as seen in the case of Herod. He had been given Philip's tetrarchy by his friend Emperor Caligula, who later added Galilee and Petrea. Politically astute, Herod then played a part in the succession of Emperor Claudius, who gave him Judea and Samaria. Herod, a powerful man, returned from Rome to administer it all.

Power so often inflates the ego. On his return, Herod's priority was his acceptance by the religious authorities and popularity with the people. He saw religious enthusiasm for the Law and Jewish religious observances as a means of gaining and keeping both. The execution of James pleased orthodox Jews, and Peter's execution would have done the same. Speaking to God of such people as Herod, the prophet Jeremiah said: 'You are always on their lips but far from their hearts.'

We know nothing of Herod's dispute with Tyre and Sidon. They wanted peace with him, but he had the upper hand: he controlled their food supplies. His decision and his inspiring speech are not recorded, but those who heard it glorified him as a god – something he did not reject. As a result of his self-importance he was immediately struck down and died.

Herod's attitude was such a contrast to the humility of Peter, Paul and Barnabas.

12:1; 21:7-15

v 1

vv 2-12
v 13

vv 15-28

12:2

Acts 10:25-26;
14:11-15

PRAYER
Dear God, in a world full of injustice remind us that when we are discouraged you will have the last word. Your justice will reign.

Singing in the night ... when discouraged

They said, 'Come, let's make plans against Jeremiah; ... let's attack him with our tongues and pay no attention to anything he says.' ... But the Lord is with me like a mighty warrior; ... Sing to the Lord! (18:18; 20:11, 13)

JEREMIAH'S life was tough! One day he was delivering clear messages from God, the next his friends and relatives were trying to stop him from speaking words which to them seemed offensive. Often, he became discouraged, disillusioned, even depressed.

Although Jeremiah belonged to a priestly family, God required him to speak against the religious and political leaders of his day. That included his relatives. But they were unable to accept him as a true prophet. They could not see things as God saw them, so they opposed Jeremiah at every turn, even threatening his life (see 11:18-19).

Jeremiah was reluctant. His sensitive nature shrank from what God wanted him to do. When he was called to be a prophet, God told him that people would not listen (see 1:4-8, 17-19), but he felt compelled to speak: '... if I say, "I will not mention his word or speak any more in his name," his word is in my heart like a fire ... in my bones. I am weary of holding it in; indeed, I cannot.'

Jeremiah had no doubt that God had called him, but sometimes he shouted at God when he met opposition. He had good grounds for feeling as he did. The message God had given to him *was* hard; the opposition *was* relentless. He felt isolated, alone, sometimes even abandoned by God. And so he complained to God: 'You deceived me ... I am ridiculed ... the word of the Lord has brought me insult and reproach all day long.' Do you ever feel like that?

When God asks us to do something for him, he knows our nature and temperament. To us his request may seem strange, even ridiculous, but God knows what he is doing. He had his own reasons for calling sensitive Jeremiah to this discouraging task; the same is true for us. The only real answer we can give is 'Yes' – and trust him for the strength, stamina, wisdom and courage we will need.

Having vented his feelings at God, Jeremiah came back to faith and trust. Our song also may include pain and anger, but can always end in trust. Try it today.

Singing in the night ... when faced with truth

'... blessed is the one who trusts in the Lord, whose confidence is in him. They will be like a tree planted by the water that sends out its roots by the stream. It does not fear when heat comes; its leaves are always green. It has no worries in a year of drought and never fails to bear fruit.' (17:7-8)

JEREMIAH'S honest dialogues with God appear with amazing regularity. It is often hard to see where the message ends and the dialogue begins. Today's reading is like that, but its message is positive: there is refreshment, strength and life for those who trust in God. Psalm 1 is uncannily similar.

The Old Testament concept of cursing (see v 5) came from a very limited, narrow understanding of God at that time. Today, as we see the full, loving nature of God in Jesus, we realise that God will never curse anyone; he loves us too much to do that. However, when we take ourselves away from the protection of his love and grace – when we look to our own wisdom instead of his – we live with the consequences and can expect not to thrive. That is our choice, not God's decision.

General John Gowans wrote this prayer: 'Without you I'll be nothing, My resources are small, Without you I'll do nothing, I'll be no use at all. Let the world wish for wisdom, ... I am asking for nothing but some more of yourself. By the power of your Spirit, ... Something more of yourself.'[11]

In London's Hampton Court Palace grounds, a very old grapevine grows in a glasshouse close to the River Thames. We are told that the vine has flourished for centuries because its roots rest in the river. A perfect illustration of the life of trust in God!

Jeremiah's dialogue with God continues with a plea for healing. The negativity and fierce opposition which he experienced almost daily had harmed his heart and worn down his spirit. He knew that he was not in a good place mentally, emotionally and in relationship with God. Constant difficulties do that to us. The coronavirus pandemic has affected us that way. Perhaps other personal difficulties and challenges have done the same.

Like Jeremiah, we too can ask God to heal us. It may take a while, especially if the harmful effects have been long and deep. Try singing Jeremiah's song – and perhaps *Salvation Army Song Book* numbers 601 ('The power of your love') or 720 ('Wonderful healer, touch me again').

Who was to blame?

When the wine was gone, Jesus' mother said to him, 'They have no more wine' (v 3)

HOW could the host have run out of wine at the wedding in Cana? This question leads us into a series on some of the miracles of Jesus. There are numerous possible answers, but our Gospel passage does not give any reason. Sometimes what the Bible doesn't say is as important as what it does say.

It could have been that the quantity needed was miscalculated, the supplier didn't provide what was ordered for whatever reason, or the bridegroom was poor or mean and ordered the minimum quantity. Was there an accident with wineskins being ruptured or jars broken? The weather could have been much hotter than normal and so guests drank more than expected. Maybe they were just greedy because the wine was free, or uninvited guests gatecrashed the wedding! Perhaps the bridegroom wouldn't accept offered help from those experienced in catering – or he did accept help, but from people incapable of doing what was needed.

The drama that unfolded can be narrowed down to three possible reasons: the bridegroom was at fault, other people were at fault, or nobody was at fault. Whatever the reason, Jesus wanted to save the day.

When it comes to helping someone, often that help is given according to whether the person is deserving or not. They are deserving if a victim of circumstances, but undeserving of help or sympathy if judged as being responsible for their situation.

How different Jesus is! It matters not how we arrive in our needy condition, Jesus offers his salvation to all. We are all undeserving of his grace. None of us deserves his sacrificial generosity, yet Christ's remedy to our spiritual poverty, whoever we are, is in place waiting to be claimed:

I have no claim on grace; I have no right to plead;
I stand before my maker's face condemned in thought
    and deed.
But since there died a Lamb who, guiltless, my guilt bore,
I lay fast hold on Jesus' name, and sin is mine no more.

SASB 463 v 1

(Albert Orsborn)

PRAYER
Dear Jesus, thank you for giving me, so undeserving, such a costly gift of grace as my salvation.

A wonder-filled wedding

... Jesus and his disciples had also been invited to the wedding (v 2)

JESUS accepted an invitation to a wedding. What a blessing to have Jesus at your wedding, and prayer is our means of inviting him to such occasions. Jesus is ever at the door awaiting an invitation – be it to a wedding, to a difficult situation we are facing, or into the hearts of each of us. He wants to be present and referred to in every aspect of our lives.

Revelation 3:20

Jesus wasn't averse to enjoying himself. He ate with and enjoyed the company of tax collectors and sinners, as well as members of the religious establishment, and at those times the menu would not have been 'locusts and wild honey'. How sad it is when Christians are considered joyless and austere. Despite sacrifice and hardships, Jesus wants us to reveal to the world the joy that he himself had.

Mark 2:15-16
Luke 7:36
Matthew 3:4

John 15:11

Mary had some sort of responsibility at the Cana wedding. When the wine ran out she brought the problem to Jesus – perhaps in a presumptuous manner, for Jesus reprimanded her. Her concern was good, and Jesus wants us to bring what troubles us to him. But when we petition the Lord, we must not presume on his response or try to control him. A day would come for that. Mary accepted the correction humbly, ordering the servants, 'Do whatever he tells you.'

God is always surprising those who obey him. The servants probably wondered why they were being told to fill the six water jars (with a total capacity of up to 720 litres) with water, when wine was what was required. But they obeyed. How shocked they must have been when they drew the water out to discover wine!

There is no way in which so much wine could have ever been consumed by that wedding party. They had already drunk all that had previously been provided. But our God is a God of superabundance who more than supplies our needs.

see also Matthew
14:13-21

PRAYER
Lord Jesus, we thank you that you are always concerned with those things which concern us. Nothing is too much for you or is ever dismissed as too trivial.

When another receives the credit

... Then he called the bridegroom aside and said, 'Everyone brings out the choice wine first and then the cheaper wine after the guests have had too much to drink; but you have saved the best till now' (vv 9-10)

THAT wedding in Cana was heading towards disaster and the bridegroom, who was responsible for provision of the wine, knew nothing about it. Had Jesus not intervened it would have been totally humiliating for the young couple and ended as a wedding no one attending would ever forget. But Jesus saved the day. How many times has the Lord stepped in and saved the day for us? There may even have been occasions when he saved us from an impending danger we were totally unaware of.

On tasting the water that had now been transformed into wine, the master of the banquet was amazed. Not only did it taste far better than the choice wine the guests had already consumed, it also broke with convention. Normal practice was to serve cheap wine after the choice wine, when the guests were less discerning. Jesus doesn't do second best, and he made it a wedding that would definitely never be forgotten. In place of humiliation the bridegroom received congratulations, the credit for it, though he knew nothing about what had happened.

The house of an ordinary Jew in Jesus' time would have consisted of one, possibly two rooms. We would call it 'open-plan'. There would be an area where food was prepared, another where it was eaten, and a sleeping area – although the family would sleep on the flat roof on very warm nights. Jesus surely watched and listened to the proceedings and was aware that credit for what he had done had been given to someone else. Yet

see Philippians 2:5-8

he said nothing. O to be like him; he who 'made himself nothing'.

> *O to be like thee! O to be like thee,*
> *Blessèd Redeemer, pure as thou art!*
> *Come in thy sweetness, come in thy fullness;*
> *Stamp thine own image deep on my heart.*

SASB 618 chorus   (Thomas O. Chisholm)[12]

PRAYER

Lord Jesus, to not get the credit for something I've done is one thing, but to see someone else receive accolades and be congratulated for it is hard to bear. I need you to do an even deeper work in my heart, that I might be more like you.

Power and authority

'Be quiet!' said Jesus sternly. 'Come out of him!' (v 25)

THE synagogue was a place of prayer and teaching. There was no music or singing. The reading of God's Word was followed by its application to daily living, which was by keeping rules and regulations created by legal experts of the past. It was all very legalistic. The scribes (teachers of the religious law) would never give an insight of their own; they always referred to the judgements of those experts.

Jesus was quite different. He spoke from the heart with an authority of his own that spoke to the heart of his listeners. He didn't back it up with the teaching of men and it amazed those who heard him. But it also disturbed one individual in the congregation. How long had that man with an impure spirit been part of that congregation? Had no one been aware of his situation?

Having laid siege to the impregnable city of Troy for 10 years, the Greeks withdrew – giving the impression they had given up the war. But they left behind a huge, hollow wooden horse as a gift. Despite warnings, the Trojans took the horse into their city and that night Greek warriors climbed out and opened the gates to the returning army, which then conquered the city.

Satan knows his best strategy against the Church is not to attack it from without but from within; to dampen the spirit, plant a spirit of evil into the membership whose hearts are not right. They may subtly blend in unnoticed, but when Jesus speaks they become uncomfortable, disturbed and even angry.

But note: Jesus didn't cast the man out of the congregation, he cast the impure spirit out of the man. Christ's power was, and still is, as amazing as his teaching.

> Purify my heart,
> Cleanse me from within and make me holy.
> Purify my heart,
> Cleanse me from my sin, deep within.
> (Brian Doerksen)[13]   SASB 517 v 2

PRAYER
Father God, create in me a pure heart, unadulterated by self-concern or self-interest, or any motive other than that of pleasing you.

Fishing with Jesus

Then Jesus said to Simon, 'Don't be afraid; from now on you will fish for people' (v 10)

John 1:40-42

THIS was not the first encounter Simon Peter and his brother Andrew had with Jesus. Andrew spent time with him on a previous occasion before introducing his brother to him. There are few greater joys this side of Heaven than that of playing a part in bringing someone to Jesus.

Here in today's incident, crowded by people wanting to hear him, Jesus chose to use Simon Peter's boat a little way from the shore as a pulpit. How wonderful it is when people are hungry to hear good preaching, but how sad when a congregation leaves as hungry as when they arrived because they were fed other than spiritual food.

Our listening to Jesus is always a prelude to working for him. When he finished speaking to the crowd, Jesus told those in the boat to let down their nets in deeper water. Christ's command sounded ridiculous and Peter as good as told him so! Daytime wasn't a time for fishing, and they were weary and discouraged having not caught a thing all night. Their nets were all clean but because it was Jesus speaking, Peter obeyed.

What then happened was mind-blowing. The haul of fish was so large that their nets began to break. When James and John then came to their aid, both boats began sinking under the weight of the catch. Did Jesus lend a hand, I wonder? Peter was humbled by it all, feeling overwhelmed and unworthy of such amazing grace. Isn't that how we sometimes feel?

But Peter had passed Christ's tests. He willingly put his boat at Christ's disposal, he obeyed when Christ's command seemed absurd, and he and his brother then left the security of their employment and new-found riches to follow Jesus.

Acts 2:41

When more than 3,000 people responded to Peter's sermon on the Day of Pentecost, did that amazing day and the words of Jesus, 'From now on you will fish for people,' come to mind?

PRAYER

When I am weary and discouraged by failure, and what you require of me seems absurd, Lord, help me not to give up but to trust and obey you.

Singing in the night ... a song of mission

The Spirit of the Sovereign Lord is on me, because the Lord has anointed me to proclaim good news to the poor. ... to bind up the broken-hearted, ... to proclaim ... release from darkness for the prisoners (Isaiah 61:1)

MISSION statements seem to be in vogue these days. Not only churches have them but also organisations, companies and even shops, to announce their purpose. None is more significant than this one from Isaiah: the mission statement of one who would restore Israel – and the mission statement of Jesus himself. Jesus declared it at the beginning of his ministry and lived it fully.

When Isaiah proclaimed it, Israel had been in exile for some time; an inevitable consequence of their consistent refusal to put God first. Now, after they had time to reflect on the failure which caused their exile – a generation of time – God saw that the nation was ready to be restored to its own land and reinstated as his people. The message gave them new hope; a second chance.

God gives us second chances – and more! We all fail at times: fail God and fail others. Ever since sin came into the world, failure has been part of being human. It restricts us, colours our judgements and leads us to focus on ourselves instead of on God and others. We call it the 'human condition' – but it is a condition we brought upon ourselves, just like Israel of Old Testament times.

God's will for us has always been the opposite: freedom, joy, love, peace, goodness – in fact, all the things listed in Galatians 5:22-23. That was why Israel was given a second chance – and it was why Jesus came.

As Isaiah shows, it is the Spirit of God who provides the mission statement, spelling out God's will for his people; and it is the Spirit of God, living within us, who enables us to live the transformed lives outlined in it. Jesus came to make us free – and loving. He wants us to be his agents in demonstrating it to others too. This can be our own mission statement, for the transformation of our own lives and for others.

Are you allowing him to transform your life – and then to equip you to bring the same truth to others? If so, the song of Isaiah, the song of Jesus, is for you to sing also.

Singing in the night ... a song of delight

I delight greatly in the LORD; my soul rejoices in my God. For he has clothed me with garments of salvation and arrayed me in a robe of his righteousness (v 10)

PARTY-TIME! After the pain and loss experienced through exile, Israel could look forward to a new era of celebration, restoration and new growth.

Psalm 137 expresses eloquently Israel's exile experience: 'By the rivers of Babylon we sat and wept when we remembered Zion. ... How can we sing the songs of the LORD while in a foreign land?' (vv 1, 4). We sense Israel's pain. But now that will end; it's time to celebrate.

Partying needs new clothes; new faces. The mourning and sadness of exile would be replaced with joy and delight; the punishment replaced with hope, restoration and salvation. Like the father of the lost son (see Luke 15:11-24), God himself would rejoice when Israel returned to him and was reinstated as his people. There was everything to celebrate.

But partying, celebration, is brief. The real work of transformation would take time. To 'rebuild the ancient ruins and restore the places long devastated' (Isaiah 61:4) does not happen overnight. Seedlings newly planted require our patience, hope and faith to grow into maturity. This restoration process would continue far into the future and take all of Israel's faith, patience and hope.

In the musical *Glory!*, John Gowans wrote: 'It's the work of a moment, It's the work of a lifetime, It begins in an instant, It may take eternity, But the work of the Spirit ... Can begin at this moment in me.' That sums it up really.

The song of delight for Israel was well justified. After 70 years in exile – 70 years to reflect on their failures – their relief must have been palpable; an explosion of joy! At the same time, Isaiah reminded them of the uphill climb ahead, as they returned to God and their homeland and began the rebuilding, regrowing, maturing process – rather like emerging after a pandemic lockdown, but much more so.

Jesus promised that mourners will find comfort, but to rebuild according to God's plan and so 'inherit the earth' requires meekness, humility, willingness to become more like him (see Matthew 5:4-5; also readings for 23 and 29 January). Let's sing the party song first, celebrating God's love, welcome and forgiveness – and then let's rebuild under his guidance.

Hoping beyond hope

'Sir,' the invalid replied, 'I have no one to help me into the pool when the water is stirred. While I am trying to get in, someone else goes down ahead of me' (v 7)

THE question Jesus asked this man, paralysed for 38 years, sounds ridiculous as well as insensitive: 'Do you want to get well?' Why wouldn't he? But on further reflection it's not as absurd as it first appears.

In his present condition the man had an affinity and probably long-term friendships with many fellow sufferers around that crowded pool. Able-bodied, he might lose those relationships. Would he be capable of making new friends? Unable to continue begging, would he be able to find employment? What skills could he offer to a prospective employer?

The pool had healing properties for the first person to enter when the waters stirred. The man explained how he did want to get well but had no one to help him into the pool. Despite his efforts, someone else always got in first.

He may have despaired of ever receiving healing, having waited in vain for decades while more-recent arrivals with milder conditions jumped in first and walked away healed. But still he was there; he had not given up. He still hoped that God would heal him. Not unlike Abraham, who 'believed and hoped, even when there was no reason for hoping...'. *Romans 4:18 GNB*

It can sometimes seem that God is blessing and answering the prayers of others while we wait longingly for him to do the same for us. Elizabeth Codner, wife of a Church of England minister, expressed something of those sentiments on hearing of the spiritual revival taking place in Ireland in the 1860s:

Lord, I hear of showers of blessing
Thou art scattering full and free,
Showers, the thirsty land refreshing;
Let some showers fall on me,
Even me, even me,
Let some showers fall on me.   *SASB 302 v 1*

PRAYER
Father God, when help is not forthcoming and it seems that others are preferred, and my hopes are dashed time and again, help me to wait on you. Give me a faith in you that will never give up.

Something worse?

'See, you are well again. Stop sinning or something worse may happen to you' (v 14)

see Luke 19:10

WE can easily live in a cocoon, a bubble, unaware of people desperate for help we could provide. Jesus came seeking out those in need. At the pool of Bethesda he sought out one man in that great crowd of broken humanity. We are not told why he chose not to heal them all.

Of all the people who lay there, how privileged the paralysed man was to have Jesus say to him, 'Get up! Pick up your mat and walk.' Jesus demanded he do the very thing he was incapable of doing; he gave him a part to play in the miracle. How often have we not done what God would have us do because we've felt incapable of doing it, unaware of the miracle God had in store?

see also Luke 17:11-19

Matthew 5:45

Possibly due to the excitement of being healed, the man let Jesus slip away without finding out who had blessed him so. He probably didn't thank him either. The Lord blesses both bad and good people, those who know him and those who don't. The difference is that we who recognise the source of our blessings are forever praising and thanking him.

On seeing the man carrying a load on the Sabbath, the Jewish leaders – somewhat like religious policemen! – were more interested in why the man was breaking their law rather than delighting in what God had done for him. I recall a church member complaining how a new convert used a swear word in a conversation following the meeting, yet I had not reprimanded him. 'You sadden me,' I replied. 'Not once have you ever spoken of the amazing thing God is doing in his life, yet the minute he slipped you couldn't wait to tell me.'

Jesus had not finished with the man at the pool and sought him a second time. 'Don't sin again in case something worse happens to you,' he told him. Can there be anything worse than the 38 years of misery he suffered? Though rarely mentioned and preached about today, the Bible says there is!

PRAYER
Jesus, make me aware of the needs of others, never forgetting that their greatest need is you and your free gift of salvation.

Touch me again

... When he had spat on the man's eyes and put his hands on him, Jesus asked, 'Do you see anything?' (v 23)

THIS miracle of Jesus is unique in that the man was *not* instantly healed. (Perhaps that is why Matthew and Luke omitted it.) Together, the details in the story give an indication as to why it wasn't an instant cure:

1. The man didn't come himself, he was brought by others.
2. He did not speak for himself, his friends spoke for him.
3. As with the deaf and mute man earlier, Jesus took the man away from any distractions. We all need to spend time alone with Jesus if we are to hear him clearly. `Mark 7:32-35`
4. Jesus spat on the man's eyes and placed his hands on him. Knowing how people in that day believed in the healing power of spittle, Jesus occasionally resorted to using it as an aid to limited faith. `see Mark 7:33; John 9:6-7`
5. Nowhere else does Jesus question whether a miracle has been completely successful as he does here.

No longer completely blind, the man still could not see clearly. People looked like trees moving about. His view of Jesus wasn't clear and his view of other people was dim. Nevertheless, he could have departed pleased that he was less likely to bump into things. However, having his sight partially restored gave him faith in what more Jesus could do for him, so he allowed Jesus to touch his eyes again. This time he 'looked intently' and saw everything clearly. `v 25 GNB`

Praise God that Mark didn't omit this miracle. For when we come to Christ he brings sight and, although we are excited at seeing what we never saw before, we soon learn that it is but the beginning. We need him to touch us again and again:

Lord, here today my great need I am feeling;
Wilt thou not visit my soul once again?
I long to feel thy sweet touch and its healing;
Wonderful healer, touch me again.

(William Henry Woulds)   *SASB* 720 v 1

PRAYER
Thank you for opening my eyes, Lord. Continue what you have begun, that I might see more clearly.

Precious to Jesus

'Daughter, your faith has healed you. Go in peace and be freed from your suffering' (v 34)

v 17

SOME people reject Jesus, others welcome him. The Gerasenes pleaded with him to leave them, but on the other side of the lake a large crowd had gathered to welcome him.

Jairus, a synagogue leader, came to Jesus deeply troubled. His 12-year-old daughter was dying. On seeing Jesus he fell at his feet pleading he come, lay hands on and heal her. Jesus agreed and went with him. Pride can so easily prevent us from humbling ourselves and pleading for help, however great our need. But Jairus was desperate and believed Jesus could and would answer his cry.

How different it was for a woman hidden in that crowd. She was too frightened and would not face Jesus. For 12 years she had suffered with continual bleeding. Society considered her unclean. A social outcast, unable even to attend worship, she had tried every avenue available for healing to no avail. In desperation she sought Jesus. How often do we come to Jesus as a last resort, when he ought to be our first port of call?

Although her sense of shame and perhaps unwillingness to interrupt Christ's more-important mission to a dying girl may have held her back, her faith was strong. She believed that by merely touching Jesus' cloak she would be healed. But we cannot keep secrets or steal blessings from God. As urgent as the little girl's need was, Jesus stopped and would not continue until he found the person who touched him.

Though fearful as to why Jesus might wish her to identify herself, the woman fell at his feet and told him the truth. The Lord loves it when we own up to what he already knows about us. How tender he was. How tender he is.

In his delay attending to the little girl and calling the woman his daughter, he revealed that no one was more precious to him than she was. What was true for her then is as true today for you and me.

PRAYER
Thank you, Jesus, for loving me and making me feel precious when I so easily feel otherwise.

Just believe

Overhearing what they said, Jesus told him, 'Don't be afraid; just believe' (v 36)

WAS Jairus frustrated by the diversion as well as the lack of any sense of urgency when Jesus continued talking with the woman after healing her? Devastating news then arrived that no parent ever wants to hear: 'Your daughter is dead.' In a flash all hope was dashed. Those who brought the message saw no point in bothering Jesus any more. Had Jesus not overheard their comments and intervened, Jairus may well have walked away. But Jesus offered Jairus hope. Man's last word is not God's last word.

When things do not work out as we hoped or expected; when we feel let down, disappointed with the Lord, he calls out to you and me – as he did Jairus: 'Don't be afraid; just believe.' Proverbs 3:5 implores us, 'Trust in the LORD with all your heart and lean not on your own understanding.'

When Jesus arrived at Jairus's home he discovered a noisy crowd of mourners already there – including flute players. see Matthew 9:23 They were probably paid mourners.

While all physical signs may have confirmed that the girl was dead, to Jesus she was only sleeping and he spoke to her as one might wake a sleeping child. The crowd laughed at what he said. The words of Jesus are often laughed at today, as are we who believe and proclaim them. Jesus was having none of it. He put out all who would quench the Spirit and just allowed those who believed him to witness what he was about to do.

When the Lord commands us to do the seeming impossible, he will always assist us as we seek to obey him. He doesn't expect us to fulfil his will without his aid. In commanding that little dead girl, 'Get up!' he took her hand to help her do so. Her recovery was not a gradual one but immediate, complete and amazing. God wants to – and can! – do the astonishing among *us* too – if we would just believe.

PRAYER
Father, when the worst happens without any visible rhyme or reason, give me the faith I need to believe and trust you in my darkness.

Singing in the night ... the song of a loving father

'I led them ... with ties of love. To them I was like one who lifts a little child to the cheek, and I bent down to feed them. ... How can I give you up, Ephraim? ... all my compassion is aroused' (vv 4, 8)

IMAGINE the scene: the father is agonising over a rebellious child, acknowledging his love for the child through the years and lamenting the child's waywardness. Perhaps you can identify with this in your own experience or family?

Through this very tender image Hosea reveals the depth of God's love for Israel. The realisation that God is loving as well as authoritative was quite new then. We can feel the depth of that love as Hosea describes God like a father holding the child's arms as they learn to walk, lifting them to his cheek, bending down to feed them.

And then the rebellious teenager appears (vv 5-7). God the Father's anger is palpable: righteous anger, not because his children have offended him but because they refuse to do what is right and good. His anger is calmed by his love and he concludes that to 'roar like a lion' may have the desired effect, turning them back to what is right, after which he will 'settle them in their homes'.

It is all there: intense love and commitment, deep righteous anger – strong but under control – and then love again. Really, it *all* is love, including the anger. Jesus turning over the money-changers' tables in the Temple (John 2:13-17) was an act of love too, very similar to Hosea's picture.

Parenthood stirs deep emotions. Sadly, for some those emotions become negative and destructive instead of loving, damaging both child and family.

Negative experiences in our own upbringing can make it hard for us to connect at depth with a loving Father-God. If that is your experience, take time to focus on God's love as described by Hosea, even though it may stir your heart with sadness. It is good to seek out another wise, experienced and caring Christian also, to support you as you bravely face your own pain and discover God's true love for you.

Take time to reflect today on God's love and its effects on your life. And pray for all parents, including those whose own negative experiences lead them to harm their children – and for those who have been on the receiving end of the pain and damage.

Singing in the night ... a song of gladness and love

'The Lᴏʀᴅ your God is with you, the Mighty Warrior who saves. He will take great delight in you; in his love he will no longer rebuke you, but will rejoice over you with singing' (v 17)

YESTERDAY we explored God's love for a wayward child – a love which included righteous anger when needed. Today's reading expresses the restoration of that relationship after punishment. It speaks of encouragement and hope: 'Sing, ... Be glad and rejoice' ... 'Do not fear, ... do not let your hands hang limp.' The Lord, the King, the Father, is here; he is not angry any more. He was never far away; there is nothing to fear (v 15). After punishment comes restoration. It is time for his child to find him again.

When we have passed through tests and challenges – when God has had to correct us perhaps, allowing difficulties to come so that we will learn his way – we may feel limp, weak, lacking motivation (v 16). When we are bruised it is easy to look down at the circumstances, instead of looking up to Jesus. Remember Peter, when he walked on the water towards Jesus (Matthew 14:25-31)?

God is in control of events. He will rescue his people and deal with the things that led them astray (vv 18-19). And then, as we saw in yesterday's reading, he will bring them home and make things right for them. Look up, not down – and let God put new courage, new strength into you as you look to him.

God's tender love has never really been lost. Imagine a father singing softly to his little child; see the reassuring smile on his face and his desire to calm and settle the child. What a beautiful picture!

Young men of a certain tribe were required to spend a night alone in the forest, to prove their courage. One was terrified, but determined to pass the test. As dawn broke, he saw a movement nearby and prepared to attack. A figure came forward. It was his father, who said, 'All night I have been behind that tree, watching over you.'

God is like that. Even when he has to discipline us, he is always nearby: watching, caring, loving. We have nothing to fear. Why not sing Zephaniah's song today, to strengthen your relationship with God?

The need of Jesus

When Jesus heard what had happened, [to John the Baptist] he withdrew by boat privately to a solitary place (v 13)

JESUS was so busy that neither he nor his disciples had eaten when news arrived that John the Baptist had been beheaded.

see Mark 6:27-31

Matthew 11:7-15

John was Jesus' cousin and highly regarded by Jesus, having given his life to preparing people for the coming of Christ. Anyone who has lost someone dear to them will empathise with Jesus' need to get away and find solitude. John's death surely brought to mind what lay ahead for Jesus too.

The crowds, unaware of his need and unwilling to let him go, followed Jesus on foot as the boat sailed along the coastline. How easy it is to come to Jesus in prayer and present him with all our problems and concerns – as he wants us to – yet fail to seek what *he* feels, *his* desires, *his* heart. What would have been our response to a crowd who just would not give us a break? Frustration? Anger? But seeing the need of the people before him, Jesus was filled with a compassion which set aside his own need, and he 'began teaching them' as well as healing 'those who were ill'.

Mark 6:34

As evening approached, Jesus could have quite reasonably sent the hungry crowd away to fend for themselves, but he didn't. Though he would not turn stones into bread for himself, he did not hesitate to use his power to feed others. Jesus always made time for people even when it cut across his own plans. He never resented interruption or made a person feel a nuisance; he never turned people away because he was too busy or had something or someone more important to attend to. Giving others the sense that we have all the time in the world for them, when actually we are hard-pressed, is as important as anything we ever say or do.

Matthew 4:2-4

John 6:37

Except I am moved with compassion,
How dwelleth thy Spirit in me?
In word and in deed burning love is my need;
I know I can find this in thee.

SASB 626 refrain

(Albert Orsborn)

PRAYER

Dear Jesus, give me a compassion that matches yours, so that others might see you in me.

He is ever watching over us

But Jesus immediately said to them: 'Take courage! It is I. Don't be afraid' (v 27)

AFTER the miraculous feeding of more than 5,000 people, Jesus wanted nothing to go to waste; the disciples filled twelve baskets with leftovers. Nothing Jesus ever does or would have us do is ever wasted, even though we may never know how he makes use of it.   *John 6:12-13*

Reluctant to leave following the miracle, Jesus *made* the disciples get into the boat and depart while he dismissed the crowd. Why the urgency? John's Gospel account tells us the people wanted to make Jesus king by force, which was not God's plan. Free at last, Jesus was able to rest awhile and pray in solitude.   *6:15*

Sometimes Jesus tests our faith, sending us on a mission when all is calm, yet knowing a dreadful storm will engulf us before we reach our destination. Will we keep going when he seems far away or will we turn back? Having watched the disciples struggling in a relentless storm, Jesus went out to meet them. He was training his disciples to understand that, however far away he may appear to be, his eye is ever on them. He is never detached from what we are going through when we live in obedience to him – even though things may appear otherwise.

The Christ who created the scientific laws that govern our planet is not subject to them. Seeing someone or something defying gravity terrified the disciples, until Jesus assured them that it was him walking on the water. Peter so wanted to be close to the Saviour he loved, if Jesus would only invite him. So he begged him, 'Tell me to come...' – and Jesus did.

'Let us keep our eyes fixed on Jesus,' says Hebrews 12:2. Courageous Peter had a firm footing while his eyes were fixed on Jesus. Only when he looked away at the danger surrounding him did his faith waver and he begin to sink. But praise God for a wonderful Saviour who reaches out to save us, aid us, even when our faith fails.   *GNB*

PRAYER
Forgive me when I've turned my eyes from you, Lord. Your eye is ever on me. Thank you for never giving up on me despite my failings.

Undeserving of grace

'Even the dogs under the table eat the children's crumbs' (v 28)

see Matthew
15:1-14

Mark 3:7-8

Matthew 15:23

ON Monday we read of Jesus' need to get away from the crowds and find solitude. Respite still eluded him. In addition, he had offended a group of Pharisees, accusing them of hypocrisy. Consequently, he travelled to Phoenicia in Syria, close to Tyre, intent on getting away from the relentless demands made on him. But there was no keeping his presence secret. He was well known even there.

One particular woman came begging him to heal her daughter. His initial response of silence was mistaken by his disciples as unwillingness to engage with her, so they wanted to 'send her away'. But (as we also saw on Monday) Jesus never turned anyone away. When he did speak, however, his words appeared shocking. While Jews contemptuously referred to Gentiles as 'dogs', how could such a derogatory word have ever left the lips of Jesus?

This is one passage where I wish I could see the expression on Jesus' face or hear the tone of his voice. Though he may well have used a milder word, that of a much-loved pet unlike the one Jews normally used, it was still insulting. But was there a hint of a smile and irony as he spoke?

'*First* let the children eat,' Jesus said. Israel was chosen by God to reveal his love and salvation to the world. God chose the Jews with the rest of us in mind. While the woman accepted the priority of the Jews, she realised Jesus wasn't excluding Gentiles like herself. She wasn't asking to sit at the table. Like a much-loved pet, she would gladly sit under the table at the feet of Jesus.

She accepted her unworthiness, grateful for a crumb compared with all that Jesus was currently giving to Jews, believing a crumb from him was all her daughter needed.

He had tested her faith which, together with her humility, understanding and wit, resulted in Jesus healing her daughter.

PRAYER
We are undeserving of any gift from you, and more blessed by crumbs from your table than anything this world has to offer. Thank you, Jesus.

Controlled by the Spirit

So when he heard that Lazarus was ill, he stayed where he was two more days (v 6)

JESUS loved Martha, Mary and Lazarus, so why did he not drop everything and rush to their home in Bethany when he heard that Lazarus was so ill? Instead, he delayed his departure for two whole days.

Some suggest he was busy baptising people, for he was in the place where John had baptised. But John 4:2 says that baptising people was something Jesus didn't do himself; he delegated it to his disciples. Another suggestion is that had he gone to Bethany as soon as he received the message, he would still have got to Lazarus too late: the delay of two days would not have made any difference to the outcome. Lazarus had been dead four days when Jesus eventually got to Bethany, and would have already been dead two days had Jesus responded immediately.

10:40

Yet the fact remains that Mary and Martha were grieving. They would have benefitted from the comfort that Jesus would bring. What minister, on hearing of the death of someone belonging to their congregation, would fail to make visiting the grieving family a priority? Surely, loving that family as he did, Jesus wanted to be there. We later see how deeply he felt for them in the tears he shed with Mary, and then at the tomb of Lazarus.

v 32-35, 38

But Jesus wasn't controlled by his emotions, the expectations of others, fear of criticism and judgement by others – or even the great compassion he had. He was controlled by the Holy Spirit: what the Holy Spirit desired and the special plan God had on this occasion. However, the disciples probably thought Jesus was being prudent, avoiding those in Judea who sought to harm him, having gone to the Jordan in the first place to escape from them. Then, after two days, Jesus alarmed his disciples by telling them he was going back to Judea – something they thought suicidal.

10:39-40

vv 8, 16

When we are led by the Spirit to do what God would have us do, he will always vindicate us – as he did Jesus, for what was in store would glorify God.

PRAYER
Holy Spirit, give me courage to obey you even when it leaves me open to being misjudged.

Setting the prisoner free

... Jesus called in a loud voice, 'Lazarus, come out!' The dead man came out, his hands and feet wrapped with strips of linen, and a cloth round his face (vv 43-44)

THAT little family in Bethany was highly respected and loved by many who came to comfort the sisters. Did God have Jesus delay so that a large crowd would be there and be witnesses to what Jesus would do?

Hearing Jesus was near, Martha couldn't wait to go and meet him, but her sister remained in the house. Why? Was she too grief-stricken or was it that she was disappointed with Jesus? Has Jesus ever disappointed you, having failed to do what you expected? Both sisters believed the Lord could have healed their brother if only he had been there. The truth is he did not need to be there to have healed Lazarus.

Although she reproached Jesus, Martha believed that God would still give Jesus whatever he asked. It did not mean she knew what that might be, for when Jesus said her brother would rise again it didn't enter her head that Jesus meant he would rise physically from the tomb. To Jesus, death was but a sleep from which a believer will be woken.

v 11

Only on hearing that Jesus was asking for her did Mary get up and hurry to him. A crowd followed her. Falling at Jesus' feet, Mary voiced the same complaint as her sister. Seeing everyone weeping, Jesus wept too. The Lord commands that we 'weep with them that weep'. It's not easy to voluntarily enter someone else's sorrow, to grieve by choice out of love for the mourner. But it is how God is: 'In all their distress he too was distressed.'

Romans 12:15 *KJV*

Isaiah 63:9

Martha was concerned Lazarus's body was already decomposing when Jesus commanded the tomb be opened. But following a prayer, Jesus commanded Lazarus, 'Come out!' and he came out – and the glory of God and the power of Jesus could not be denied by anyone present. Our Lord still commands, 'Come out', to those dead in their sin and has the power to set the prisoner of sin and death free.

PRAYER
Jesus, I thank you for saving me, bringing me out of darkness into your light – and setting me free.

Singing in the night ... a song of anguish and trust

**Jesus cried out in a loud voice, ... 'My God, my God, why have you forsaken me?' ...
'Father, into your hands I commit my spirit' (Matthew 27:46; Luke 23:46)**

EASTER is almost here! To help us prepare, we consider today the most precious song of all: the song of Jesus. It is almost too sacred for comment – and yet, perhaps Jesus would want us to reflect on his own 'song in the night'.

On the Cross, Jesus used words from Psalm 22:1 and Psalm 31:5. (We have mentioned Psalm 22 in earlier readings: 23 January and 13 February.) In his day, Jewish schoolchildren were required to learn much by heart, especially scriptures and psalms. As the psalms were the Jewish song book at that time, it is not surprising that Jesus turned to them to express his feelings.

The horror and desolation of Jesus' cry: 'Why have you forsaken me?' is haunting. When he most needed support from his Father, he felt totally abandoned, as if God had turned his back on his Son – in shame. And yet, is there something different here?

Jesus knew that his crucifixion was an essential part of his mission. He had to die – and in such a public, humiliating way – because he was carrying our sin on his own shoulders. In that moment he felt *our* separation from God as if it were *his*; and, his own relationship with the Father being so close, his agony was even stronger than ours would have been.

But that was not the end! If you grew up in The Salvation Army – or any other church – you may still remember today some of the songs and choruses you sang in Sunday school, just as Jesus knew some psalms. It is thought that Psalm 31 might have been the prayer which Jewish children repeated at bedtime. Could it be that, at point of death, Jesus prayed the nightly prayer of his childhood; a prayer of total trust and rest? What a precious thought!

The bedtime prayer followed the prayer of anguish. In the midst of suffering there was total trust in God. As we read Jesus' intimate prayers – the songs in his night of greatest need – we are on holy ground again. Can we learn from him today how to handle our own greatest pain?

The risen Christ and his people: Luke's story

A series for Easter by guest writer Major Grant Sandercock-Brown

GRANT was a high school music teacher in Australia for 10 years before he and his wife Sharon entered The Salvation Army's school for officer training in Sydney in 1999. As officers they have spent 17 years in corps ministry (church leaders) and three years on the staff of Eva Burrows College where, at the time of writing this series, Grant is a lecturer.

As well as a BMusEd and a graduate diploma from Birmingham School of Music, Grant has an MA from Morling College and he completed a Doctor of Ministry at Asbury Theological Seminary.

He started writing after a successful fight with Hodgkin's disease and since then has had articles in Salvation Army publications around the world. His first book, From a Middle-aged Dad to a Teenage Daughter, *was published by International Headquarters; his second,* 21 Questions for a 21st-Century Army, *followed in 2014, published by the Australia Eastern Territory.*

Grant and Sharon have three adult children.

Introducing this set of devotions, Grant writes:
THE story of Jesus' life, death and resurrection is our central story as Christians. It is the story that gives our lives meaning and shapes our day-to-day living as well as our destiny. It is the story that binds us together as God's people. So, we need to tell this story to ourselves and to the world again and again. And there is no better time than Easter to do so.

In this series we will focus on Luke's telling of the story, starting with the triumphant entry into Jerusalem and finishing with Jesus' final words to his disciples.

My prayer is that as you engage with the daily readings, you will encounter the risen Christ in a new and refreshing way, through the Holy Spirit, and be drawn closer to the Father's heart.

How could we not know?

'I tell you,' he replied, 'if they keep quiet, the stones will cry out' (v 40)

'GO and get a donkey!' Perhaps one of Jesus' strangest requests. Regardless, two disciples obeyed. They had been journeying with Jesus, learning the value and cost of obedience to him. So, they mounted Jesus on a donkey, unleashing a moment of exuberant joy, shouting out all they'd seen, what they believed about Jesus.

I wonder if Jesus felt that his followers needed this moment with all that lay ahead. Or perhaps because of all that lay behind. Either way, on that first Palm Sunday the disciples and the crowd proclaimed more than they knew: 'Blessed is the king!' Perhaps Jesus laughed at their exuberance before he wept over Jerusalem.

If we'd been with Jesus on this journey to Jerusalem, we would get it too. His stories of the penitent tax collector and faithful servants. His welcoming the children and healing the blind. Is it any wonder that Jesus told the rebuking Pharisees that the 'rocks would cry out'? It is blindingly obvious, even to impersonal creation, that Jesus is the King. Could you and I have followed him, seen and heard him, and not proclaimed him King?

In Heaven, I'd like to sit down for a chat with some of the disciples. The background ones like Bartholomew and Thaddaeus (everybody will be chasing Peter, James and John). Or maybe talk to the donkey-fetchers. Ask them: Did you know? Did you throw the first cloak? Why did you shout? What did you mean?

They didn't know it all, but they knew he was their King, knew they had to offer him their lives. They'd discovered that the more they followed him, the more they listened to him, they more they spoke with him, the more their lives were changed. Jesus had imprinted them, made them his own.

Jesus was and is the King! He is our King, who offers us salvation, who suffers with us and for us, who weeps over us and loves us. How could you and I not know that? Rejoice!

The authority of Jesus

'Tell us by what authority you are doing these things,' they said. 'Who gave you this authority?' (v 2)

THE entry to Jerusalem had been big. But Jesus wasn't finished yet. He went to the Temple, drove out those profiting from faith, and taught every day with people hanging on every word. His enemies, alarmed, wanted to destroy him, so they attacked not his words but his right to speak. 'By what authority do you do these things?' they challenged. It's a common ploy still. When in doubt (and the priests were), undermine credibility.

Jesus answered with an even better question. He narrowed it down to a choice between heavenly or human authority, and took the question back to John the Baptist, who had foretold Jesus' ministry. John had said, 'One who is more powerful than I will come' (Luke 3:16). And he had. Jesus' enemies were caught either way, so they said, 'We don't know.'

They were so focused on Jesus' destruction that they missed his message. Jesus was proclaiming good news! But his enemies were not going to give up and would ask their question over and over in the week to come.

It's a question we are asked too: 'By what authority?' Does the proclaimer's authority come from ordination? Commissioning? Position? Popularity? 'What right do you have to tell me Jesus is the King?' we're asked. The answer is, 'None really.' Like Jesus with his enemies, we can't make people hear.

But we can bear witness to Jesus' power, just as Luke does in his Gospel. We can testify to our own encounter with Jesus. Preacher extraordinaire Fred Craddock's book on preaching is titled *As One Without Authority*.[14] It's also a job description. No, we can't 'lay down the law' like Jesus' enemies. But in Sidney Cox's words, we can 'tell out the sweet story' (*SASB* 200).

It's why we celebrate Holy Week year after year. To find ourselves again in our central story. So that, reminded, we can testify to our encounter with our Lord. That's our job this Easter, to tell the story and to tell it well to all who will listen in the hope that all will hear.

Wicked tenants

'Then the owner of the vineyard said, "... I will send my son, whom I love"' (v 13)

IT'S a story within a story. Jesus' parable of the wicked tenants is in the middle of Luke's Holy Week story. And it is a pretty obvious parable told directly after the questioning of Jesus' authority. He aimed this straight between the eyes of his enemies. Israel is the vineyard and the servants the prophets. God is the owner – and the religious leaders? They are the wicked tenants.

In the middle of the story is the owner's poignant question and answer: 'What shall I do? I will send my son, whom I love.' In a way it seems counterintuitive. Why would the owner take the risk? Why send a beloved son into danger? But the owner does, and the beloved son dies. It's a shock, of course. 'Heaven forbid!' the listeners cry, not realising that this was Heaven's work.

However, in Jesus' story there is a twist. This story is deeply connected to the Song of the Vineyard in Isaiah 5. There the vineyard is destroyed. Here it is given away to new tenants. It is a new era. There is a new immovable reality, the cornerstone that was rejected (v 17) would, as Noel Paul Stookey sang in 'Building Block', become 'the cornerstone of a whole new world'.

That's what the dire prediction in verse 18 is about. In the coming of the beloved son everything would change, everything would be broken to pieces, everything crushed. The cornerstone meant a new reality, no matter what his enemies did.

I like to think that when Jesus looked at his hearers – the disciples who loved him, the crowd who followed him, the leaders who despised him – in his stark warning there was also an appeal. Jesus' message was, 'You reject me, but can't you see that I am what you need?' Soon, and very soon, they would all need to choose.

The widow's mite

'... but she out of her poverty put in all she had to live on' (v 4)

JESUS had just beaten his opponents at their own game, outwitting them in discussions about marriage and taxes. We might think that in the contrast between the poor widow's sacrifice and the rich man's easy giving he now turns to the smallness of their hearts: 'Don't be like the rich be like the widow.' But this was a warning directed at the disciples.

Yes, the hearts of the banqueters – the teachers and their rich friends – were probably small and mean. But what the disciples needed to see and avoid was a structure where these privileged men were central and the poor, sacrificing widow was marginalised. Elsewhere, Jesus denounces the religious leaders as hypocrites full of wickedness (Matthew 23:27-28). His observations here do the same thing.

Sometimes we are hypocrites and we know it. And that's bad. But sometimes we are hypocrites and we don't know it. And that's worse. And this destructive, unrealised hypocrisy hurts people, particularly those on the margins. The elite were blind hypocrites, ensuring their own place and prestige in a system that devoured widow's houses.

There is a visible injustice here that Jesus wants his followers to see. The rich seemingly give much and the widow gives a pittance when we know that the rich give the pittance and the widow gives her all. The system doesn't even notice her, her poverty or her sacrifice.

This is called 'privilege'. And the thing about privilege is that we usually cannot see it in ourselves. The deep problem here for the rich and the rulers is not that their propositions about God were wrong, or they were not generous, but that they were central in a system that was deeply flawed – and they couldn't see it.

Something had gone wrong for the people of God. We might claim that it has gone right ever since, but we know that for a lie. Too often the people of God have created, or at least profited from, structural injustice that will keep the widow poor and marginalised, however faithful she may be.

Jesus hadn't come just to change hearts; he had come to change everything.

The Last Supper

And he said to them, 'I have eagerly desired to eat this Passover with you before I suffer' (v 15)

WHAT an extraordinary and personal moment in the middle of a cosmic event: 'I've eagerly desired to eat this meal with you.' 'This is it,' Jesus is saying. 'I won't eat again until it is finished. But I eat this meal, now, with you.' A meal redolent with historic symbolism, but more importantly, a simple meal in which Jesus shared himself with his followers and friends.

Salvationists have an awkward history with this text and its possible implications. Virtually all other Christians have wanted to re-enact this moment again and again in myriad ways, seeing something very important in its symbolism and its practice. The Salvation Army has chosen otherwise.

Still, the power and poignancy of the moment remains: 'I eagerly desired this.' Was it, in part at least, a final earthly moment of ordinariness that Jesus was enjoying? Because that's what it was. Soon the story would become singular and vast. But for now, it was common and small. A simple meal with dear friends, ordinary wine and ordinary bread. Its pathos seen only by those, like us, who know what lies ahead.

Jesus knew too, of course. And he wanted them to understand that the events of the next three days were all for them. The agony and the injustice, the glory and the hope, were all for their sake. Self-giving, unconditional love poured out. And he wanted them to remember that fact. So, he tied the remembering to a simple everyday act of breaking bread together: 'Do this in remembrance of me.' Or if you like, 'Never forget me!' In all the ordinariness of life, never forget Jesus.

I wonder if this precious memory sustained the disciples in the days and years ahead, that in looking back they realised Jesus had known their weaknesses, typified in their desertion of him, but loved them anyway. 'Remember our last supper together?' they would ask each other. They remembered that he delighted in their presence just as they did in his; that it was personal; that they felt, and would always feel, his love for them. What an extraordinary ordinary meal. What a remembering!

A redeeming reality

... and darkness came over the whole land ... for the sun stopped shining (vv 43-44)

CHURCH father John Chrysostom believed that 'we live in a world mortally wounded by sin'. He, like us, had only to look around him to a world where there was so much obvious wickedness and corruption, let alone hidden evils in people's hearts. What did God see, I wonder? Did he nod his head in agreement with Chrysostom as he wrote those words?

Since the Creation God had looked on a sinful and pain-wracked world. But we were not to be left alone in our sin. God rolled up his metaphorical sleeves, brushed the metaphorical tears from his all-seeing, love-filled eyes, and set about the process of restoration. To paraphrase the famous words in John's Gospel: God loved all of mortally wounded humanity so much that he gave of himself by sending his Son, so that our mortal wounds could be transformed into life eternal that begins here and now.

Calvary is a gift to us. We know that looking back. Although, I wonder how the angels felt, what they saw, on that first Good Friday. Were they in awe? Had God told them the plan? Did they know? Did the heavenly host hold its collective breath as God in Christ took into his very being corruption, evil, hate and death as the Godhead experienced brokenness for the first time and in that moment changed sin and mortality into forgiveness and eternity?

As the sun stopped shining and darkness covered the land, did the heavenly host then see God's boundless, redeeming love flow back through time, back through Isaiah, back through Elijah, through David, Moses, Abraham and Adam? Flow forward through history through John, and Peter and Paul, and Augustine and Aquinas, and Wesley, and Booth – to you and me? So that we can sing, always, 'Here in the death of Christ I live' (*SASB* 861 v 2). A particular death, Christ's death. This singularity, this eternal moment, which became an eternal redeeming reality.

Jesus, our Saviour, is the Lamb of God who takes away our sin, who takes corruption and death and evil and brokenness into himself. And he transforms it all and redeems it all – and in doing so the great healing is begun.

In between the times

Then they went home and prepared spices and perfumes. But they rested on the Sabbath (v 56)

AT one level the Easter narrative is a simple story. The bare facts are these: an innocent man, beaten and in pain, died an undeserved death at the hands of the State while his mates fled and the women in his life looked on. That's a story the world has seen many times. And at that level it's completely straightforward.

Of course, Jesus wasn't just a man, he was also the Son of God. But that's not all. He died willingly, having said he would 'rise again' (Luke 18:33). However, did the women who witnessed his death understand all that? As they ground spices with tears in their eyes, did they know it would be alright? As they tried to get some rest, waiting for Saturday to end, replaying over and over again Jesus' death, his cries from the cross, did they have any inkling of the Resurrection? Did they believe, or even hope, that the story wasn't finished?

It's hard to live between the times. We know something of it, I think. As Christians living in a world wounded by sin we long for, and pray for, the Kingdom to come! We long for the righteousness of God to prevail, for his redeeming love to fill and transform every heart. But that day has not yet arrived.

So, we prepare, and we rest, and we prepare, and we rest. But sometimes our preparations seem to make no difference and our resting is not enough. We can grow tired, disillusioned even, ministering between the times. It isn't easy to serve suffering humanity. The needs of the world, both global and local, can feel overwhelming.

We have an advantage over those grief-filled women on that first Easter Saturday. We've encountered God's resurrection power. Their stories' endings, like ours, are not yet written. All our life stories are in the infinitely tender hands of a God who carries us as we walk into the world he loves.

So, we prepare and we rest, knowing that the author and finisher of our faith has not finished with us yet.

At the tomb

... the women took the spices they had prepared and went to the tomb (24:1)

THE women, very early, went to find Jesus. Instead, they found an empty tomb and two angels with extraordinary news: 'He is not here, he has risen!' The women came back and told the men, but they were not believed. Peter, however, wanted to check for himself. John's Gospel tells us what happened when he did so. Mary Magdalene followed him back to the tomb.

Mary is very important in the Easter story. She's not a reformed fallen woman. Nothing in Scripture says that she is. Rather, she is the most named non-family member, her name is always listed first when with other women, and she's one of the three most-named Jesus followers. And this story tells us why.

Mary loved Jesus. She had cared for Jesus in life and was determined to do so in death. So, she stood in tears at the empty tomb. We know what follows. Jesus asked her, 'Why are you crying?' She replied, 'They have taken my Lord away,' and she turned to face him. Then, in that short conversation, Jesus says her name and she knows him.

'Go,' says Jesus, 'and tell them.' And she does. Mary was the very first person to bear witness to the risen Lord! The first sent one and the first to declare what is no longer doctrine, 'He is risen', but rather testimony, 'I have seen the Lord!'

If the cry of humanity's fall in the first garden was God's – 'What have you done?' (see Genesis 3:13) – the cry of our lifting up in this garden is Mary's – 'I have seen the Lord!' Her witness is both personal and universal. Mary is changed and everything has changed.

Mary, apostle to the apostles, probably wasn't thinking of all that as she hurried back to her friends. But she knows what she knows! Jesus is alive and everything feels different now. We can imagine Charles Wesley's words on her lips, and our lips too: 'There for me the Saviour stands ... I know, I feel, Jesus lives and loves me still' (*SASB* 457).

A personal journey

... Jesus himself came up and walked along with them (v 15)

ONE wise writer in the field of children's ministry insisted that a child's coming to faith was not one decision for Christ, but rather many decisions towards Christ. These decisions, the outcome of Christian nurture, lead to a moment when a child says, for themselves, 'Jesus loves me this I know'.[15]

This concept of a growing awareness of Christ matters. For many of us, coming to faith was not the dramatic crisis moment of Paul on the Damascus Road, but rather a lifelong journey of growing awareness of God. Some of us are unable to remember a time when we have not known him. On that road to Emmaus these two disciples lived this story.

We assume they were leaving Jerusalem because it was all over. 'We had hoped,' (past tense) they said. But Jesus walked with them and eventually they recognised him. 'Were not our hearts burning within us?' they asked. And here too is the truth of faith: often we only recognise Christ's presence in our lives looking back. It is in remembering that we clearly see God's providential care.

An 18th-century priest, Jean-Pierre de Caussade, called this 'the sacrament of the present moment'. He believed that because we can see God's providence looking back, we can always trust God to be with us in the present moment and therefore we should seek his presence. Caussade believed that if we are brave enough to fully surrender to God, every moment can be a kind of 'communion with his love'.[16] It's a simple and profound idea.

It's not new, of course. We can hear it in our own songs: 'Do you rest each moment in the crucified?' (*SASB* 421) we ask; 'Trusting as the moments fly ... trusting Jesus, that is all,' (*SASB* 892) we declare. The disciples on the road to Emmaus remind us that the risen Christ walks with us on life's journey, even when we are fleeing Jerusalem. And so, in full surrender, we too can 'trust and obey' (*SASB* 690).

The shape of worship

They asked each other, 'Were not our hearts burning within us ...?' (v 32)

THE story of the road to Emmaus speaks to more than just our personal journey of faith. It also speaks to the community of faith and our worship. Writers on worship have pointed to the four-fold pattern of Christ-centred worship: Gathering, Word, Response, Sending.[17] And this story is shaped by such a structure.

On the Emmaus road the risen Christ drew his disciples in, then he taught them from the Scriptures. This led to their response to him and to their eyes being opened. The reality and power of this encounter then sent them back to Jerusalem to tell of 'what had happened on the way' (v 35).

This is the shape of all worshipful encounter. The risen Christ walks among his people. And when we meet in his name, we are gathered by him. We are then shaped by his Word. Through the Spirit we respond to that shaping and are then sent out into the mission field. In four-fold worship we remember and retell what God has done in Christ. It is in this remembering and retelling that we are renewed.

Those of us who are worship leaders sometimes misunderstand our role, think the congregation is the audience and we are the players, and God, through his Spirit, a prompter. No, God is the audience, the congregation is the player, and the worship leader is merely a prompter. Our worship is offered to God, not to each other. It's him we seek and him we please, for then we are renewed.

Worship does not always feel like a sacred encounter with the risen Christ. There are perhaps many personal reasons for that: worry, distraction, familiarity, pride or fear. It may be the fault is not ours but rather that the worship leaders have misunderstood their role. We know performance and preference can sometimes get in the way of genuine encounter. Still, the solution lies with us. You see, it appears our Lord is courteous. On the Emmaus road 'Jesus continued on as if he were going further'. He waited for Cleopas and his companion's invitation. In worship Jesus awaits our invitation and meets us there.

Jesus appears

'Look at my hands and my feet. It is I myself!' (v 39)

A RISEN Christ is the cornerstone of the Christian faith but it's a contentious one. Millions more might find our faith acceptable if it wasn't tied to a miraculous resurrection. Some downplay the awkwardness by saying it doesn't matter if it's not true, they separate the Christ of faith from the Jesus of history. The risen Christ then becomes an abstract idea rather than the real body of the resurrected Lord his followers felt and touched. But there's no biblical warrant to deny its truth. Every New Testament witness clearly believed in the Resurrection.

In today's reading Jesus, in the flesh, appeared to his followers. In the original language it's emphatic: 'I myself.' And it is the resurrected Christ who changes everything. Just as it changed Mary and changed Cleopas and his companion. The Resurrection turned them around then and it does the same for us now.

The great danger is not so much our doubt in the miraculous. Even the disciples had 'doubts rise in [their] minds' (v 38). It's rather that we may think of God as too small; constrain our belief to something we can understand. We must not do this. If God cannot raise his beloved Son from the dead, how can he be the author of salvation? How can he be the Creator, Governor and Preserver of all things? Jesus' death and resurrection force us to decide. Will we accept the mystery and believe?

Imagine the chaos of the disciples' thoughts as they saw this speaking-and-eating Jesus. Imagine the wonder, the mystification, the questions, the hope, the awe. We can still feel its echoes; indeed, feel it for ourselves. Jesus is alive. He is alive in our hearts – or, if you like, we are alive in him. We are caught up in his heart, drawn into his resurrection life, drawn into the love of Christ. And that is mystery indeed.

Charles Wesley wrote: 'Alive in him, my living head, and clothed in righteousness divine' (*SASB* 241). May we live each day in that truth.

Unbelief, joy and amazement

They gave him a piece of broiled fish, and he took it and ate it in their presence (vv 42-43)

WHAT was it like to stand in the physical presence of the resurrected Jesus and to watch him eat a piece of fish? 'Touch me and see,' he said (v 39). I think it was incomprehensible. Hence the coexistence of their joy and their doubts. After two thousand years we are still contemplating all this moment means.

The Undoing of Death is the name of a book and sermon by Fleming Rutledge.[18] She unpacks this extraordinary idea that death is now defeated. She calls death 'the last enemy ... of God'. But through the power of God, death is now conquered. Yes, it still exists but it is no longer ultimate. The light has come into the world.

As humans we have ultimate questions: 'Is this all there is? Sorrow? Hardship? Suffering? Is death the end?' But because of the undoing of death we can answer, 'No, never again!' For the eternal Light has come, and 'in him was life, and that life was the light of all mankind ... and the darkness has not overcome it' (John 1:4-5).

Of course, we accept the reality of death. We do not hide from it or camouflage it. But we know it for a defeated enemy. 'Where, O death, is your sting?' (1 Corinthians 15:55) Paul would ask. And the answer was, 'It is no more.'

It's on this absolute, this cornerstone, that the people of God have lived. 'And the Church of Christ was born, and the Spirit lit the flame,' we sing[19] – and so we should! From that moment on, Jesus' followers faced death and suffering and an unknown future with courage and hope.

We too must live victoriously. We do not give in. We do not give up. Nothing can separate us from the love of God and his resurrection power. Nothing can separate us from the transforming, powerful, death-defeating, pain-redeeming love of God.

We live with our eyes open, our hearts filled with joy, in absolute hope. Suffering is redeemed. Hope is restored. Death is undone.

Bearing witness to a risen Lord

'… and you will be my witnesses' (v 8)

I WONDER what tone of voice Jesus used in this encounter. Was it a voice of stern command? Was it a voice of gentle comfort? Or was it a voice of warmth and pride? 'You will receive power … and you will be my witnesses.' I like to think it was the latter, for surely Jesus was proud of his followers, was smiling encouragingly at them as he spoke. They had come so far and experienced so much. And they had done well.

They had remained. They were faithful. Despite temporary desertion and paralysing doubts, here they were with their Lord still. Sure, to the world they might have seemed like a ragtag bunch of working-class nobodies. But the world would be wrong to see them as such. Their lives and their witness would eventually shake the empire itself.

I like to think that this wasn't really a command at all but rather a description of a new reality: 'You will be my witnesses, there is no other way.' They had been irrevocably transformed by all they had seen and heard, and witness was now inevitable. How could these apostles not proclaim? How could they not be more loving?

To witness extraordinary sacrifice and power, to be caught up in this great salvation story, was to be changed forever. Their families and neighbours would see this evident change and so the Kingdom would come. Sure, not in its fullness, but the Kingdom of God was within them. They took the Kingdom with them as ambassadors for their King.

And of course, their story is our story too. Jesus looks at those of us who know him with warmth and pride and says, 'You will be my witnesses, it's inevitable.' Our encounter with redeeming love cannot be ignored or hidden. We too are changed.

Yes, the depths of that mystery are unfathomable. 'Your life is now hidden with Christ in God,' Paul would say (Colossians 3:3). But its outworking is no mystery at all. We love our God and we love our neighbour – and we love because he first loved us.

We thank Grant for guiding our thoughts on this journey to the Cross, the Resurrection and through the life-changing events that followed. – *P.M.*

Singing in the night ... a song of comfort (1)

Comfort,... my people, says your God. Speak tenderly to Jerusalem, and proclaim to her that her hard service has been completed, that her sin has been paid for ... He tends his flock like a shepherd: he gathers the lambs in his arms and carries them close to his heart (vv 1-2, 11)

HOME TIME! God's people have been in exile in Babylon for around 70 years, away from their home country, because they had refused to follow God's way (see Jeremiah 25:1-5, 8-11 and 29:4-7, 10). Now it is time for their restoration and return after years of hardship and pain.

Isaiah reminds them of God's nature, power and love. People come and go, like grass and flowers, but God's word stands for ever. God knows the exact amount of water in the oceans, lakes and rivers. He knows the size and weight of every mountain – and the amount of dust on the earth! God knows *everything*. Therefore, of course, he knows every detail of them and their lives also.

God is greater than all other gods. He will act in power on their behalf, but will treat them gently, in great love. It must have been hard for them to believe this at first, after their exile years; overwhelming, perhaps.

In Babylon, a whole generation of them had lived among people who worshipped other gods. Their younger people had known *only* Babylon. Under such circumstances it was easy for them to be pulled away from what they had been taught; to become confused; to be influenced by lifestyles and patterns which were alien to the ways of God.

It's not that they intentionally followed other ways – although some might have made that choice; it's just that the constant daily contacts may have weakened their faith by offering instant satisfaction and solace. The same can happen to us, too, in a world which does not acknowledge God.

But now the real, true solace, from God himself, is coming to them. In comparison with God, all other nations – including Babylon (and all other ideologies and lifestyles) – are powerless, like a drop of water in a bucket or dust on weighing scales.

'Do not be afraid,' says Isaiah. 'Do not feel overpowered by Babylon. *This* is your God. He is coming to deliver and restore you. Get ready!' What a great song to sing! How it must have instilled new hope in Judah. What does it say to you, in your situation, today?

Singing in the night ... a song of comfort (2)

Why do you say,... 'my cause is disregarded by my God'? ... those who hope in the LORD ... will soar on wings like eagles; they will run and not grow weary, they will walk and not be faint (vv 27, 31)

PERHAPS God's people needed a lot of persuasion to believe that he was really going to send them home at last, after so long in exile! Isaiah certainly goes to great lengths to convince them of God's greatness.

Clearly some of them did *not* know; had *not* heard – or was it perhaps that they doubted what they had heard? Their priests would have tried to teach them and hold them to their faith, but the surrounding influences would have been great, especially for the new generation who had been born in exile.

So, Isaiah paints a powerful picture: 'To whom can you compare God? Certainly not with other gods! *Your* God created even the stars – and knows each of them by name!' (see vv 25-26).

Isaiah's description of God is thrilling; it also puts God's people firmly in their place. It is as if Isaiah is saying:

'Do you *really* think that you can trifle with God – or that the gods of other nations have any power at all? No! Their gods are just man-made. Your God is the only true God; the only one with any real power – and the only one who cares about you. You are a privileged people because you are his.
'It is time to let go of the negative thinking and doubts which have dogged your steps for so long. Look to God, lift up your heads and hearts – and let him show you who he *really* is.
'You who knew the old life in your homeland; remember. Young people who know only Babylon; listen and learn. *This* is your God. He is coming to rescue and restore you. A new life is just ahead – and God will give you strength to reach it.'

Does Isaiah's message touch a chord in your heart? Take a moment now to consider your own understanding of God. Does it equal the picture Isaiah paints – or does it fall short? Perhaps today is the time to ask God to show you more of who he really is – and to give you new strength and trust, so that you can sing Isaiah's song.

God desires our good

'The LORD bless you and keep you; the LORD make his face shine on you and be gracious to you; the LORD turn his face towards you and give you peace' (vv 24-26)

IN an excavation in 1979 in Ketef Hinnom, near Jerusalem, two tiny silver scrolls, thought to have been worn as amulets, were discovered. When unrolled, they revealed the oldest portion of Scripture found outside the Bible – today's key text. This blessing has out-survived all other Scripture of that period!

God told Moses that the priests, God's intermediaries or intercessors, were to declare this particular blessing to his people. According to the Mishnah (the first major written collection of the Jewish oral traditions known as the Oral Torah) it was used by priests in temple worship. The words in Hebrew make it clear that it is a blessing God has for each of his people – including you and me today.

God wishes to bless us. He desires our good and not our harm. He desires to keep us – keep us safe, secure and healthy in his love, providing all we need. He desires to keep us close to him as a mother hen 'gathers her chicks under her wings', though he can only do that if we let him.

Luke 13:34

God wishes to shine his face on us, casting away all shadows, removing the darkness, and ensuring that we do not live under a cloud. Jesus promised us 'life in all its fullness'.

John 10:10 *GNB*

God wishes to turn his face towards us, not away, that we might see it glowing in pleasure, not glowering displeased; that we might sense his smile and feel we are accepted, loved, forgiven. For in that experience we find his peace – *shalom*. The Hebrew and the Greek equivalent of *shalom* means completeness, wholeness, soundness, well-being. It is a gift God gives to those who put their trust in him.

> We have peace, peace with God, ...
> By God's love, by God's grace, we may look on his face;
> We have peace, perfect peace with God.

SASB 524

(Howard Davies)

PRAYER
Father God, thank you that you have such love for each one of us, your children. Lord, make us worthy of your blessings.

Peace beyond our understanding

Now may the Lord of peace himself give you peace at all times and in every way (v 16)

THE peace, the *shalom*, we mentioned yesterday is something every human heart longs for. Epictetus, a first-century pagan thinker, said, 'While the Emperor may give peace from war on land and sea, he is unable to give peace from passion, grief and envy. He cannot give peace of heart, for which man yearns more than ever he does for outward peace.'

Isaiah 9:6 described Jesus as the coming Prince of Peace. Even in a raging storm that terrified his disciples, Jesus was at peace – asleep in the boat! To Jesus, such a life-threatening experience was not a cause for losing the peace he possessed. As he approached Calvary and the end of his earthly life, he told his followers not to have troubled hearts or be afraid. He was giving them his peace – a peace within – something very different to that which the world might offer.   Mark 4:37-38 / John 14:27

Paul spoke of that peace as surpassing, or transcending, all understanding. Our outward circumstances may be terribly turbulent, disturbing and upsetting, but still, deep within our hearts, there is the assurance of 'peace with God'.   Philippians 4:7 / Romans 5:1

It was that peace which sustained Horatio Spafford and his wife following the tragic drowning of their four daughters, whereby Horatio, despite tremendous grief, could write the moving words:

> When peace like a river attendeth my way,
> When sorrows like sea billows roll,
> Whatever my lot, thou hast taught me to know
> It is well, it is well with my soul.   *SASB* 741 v 1

The peace that God gives isn't an absence of trouble or difficulty which one might normally associate with peace, which is why it is described as being beyond human understanding. We can be weeping with sorrow, bereft of much that is dear to us, and yet have a deep sense that God knows what he is about and can be trusted whatever befalls us. It tells of God's promise to us: 'Thou wilt keep him in perfect peace, whose mind is stayed on thee: because he trusteth in thee.'   Isaiah 26:3 / *KJV*

PRAYER
Jesus, give me that stillness in the storm, that trust in you which brings forth the peace you promised.

Love beyond measure

... And I pray that you, being rooted and established in love, may have power, together with all the Lord's holy people, to grasp how wide and long and high and deep is the love of Christ (vv 17-18)

KNOWING Christ is a very personal thing. It is knowledge based on experience gained in a relationship. There is knowledge in the form of knowing the Bible, knowing and accepting the gospel truths as facts which, whilst both worthwhile and enriching, is not what Paul is speaking of in this passage.

see also
Philippians 3:7-10

We might know all the facts about a person, having read numerous biographies and perhaps followed them on social media, yet still not know them personally. Paul yearned that God's people would be strengthened by the Holy Spirit's powerful presence to know Christ's presence in their hearts.

Ephesians 1:20;
Romans 8:34;
Colossians 3:1

Jesus sits at the right hand of the Father in Heaven, but the Holy Spirit brings the reality of his presence into our inner being. This is why we speak of both the Holy Spirit and Jesus being in our hearts in an interchangeable way.

Like a sapling planted in enriching soil, we must be rooted and established in the love of Christ. If a sapling isn't rooted and established it will easily become victim to strong storms. Deeply rooted and well established, it may take a battering but the power of the storm will not prevail; the sapling will still be standing when the clouds part to reveal the sun again.

John 13:34
Colossians 3:13

The source of us loving others as Christ loved us and forgiving others as Christ forgave us, as we are commanded to, is only to be found in Christ himself. We cannot conjure up the supernatural limitless love and forgiveness needed. We can only share the love of Christ that we experience. Without being rooted in it, the love we have will always be limited and require effort as we try to match what God requires.

None the love of Christ can measure,
None its depths can ever tell.
None can estimate the treasure
Held by those who with him dwell.

SASB 880 v 1   (Richard Slater)

PRAYER
Thank you, Lord Jesus, for the enormous, immeasurable love you show to me. Rooted in you, may others see that love in me.

To God be the glory

Now to him who is able to do immeasurably more than all we ask or imagine, according to his power that is at work within us, to him be glory in the church and in Christ Jesus throughout all generations, for ever and ever! Amen (vv 20-21)

GOD never disappoints. If we ask and expect little we receive little, but if we ask and expect great things of God we are in for surprises. God is able to do more than all we ask or imagine.

Grateful to God for what he had already done in making him king, Solomon was focused on being the king God desired. When God asked him what he wanted, Solomon requested that the wisdom and knowledge he needed for the task would be given rather than the things most people hanker for. In response, God gave him far more than he asked or imagined. *see 2 Chronicles 1:7-12*

But our prayers, like Solomon's, need to revolve around God and what he desires. He is not there merely to supply what we want, need or think best. In fact, our Father knows what our needs are 'before we ask him'. Prayer can so easily degenerate into a long shopping list whereby God is treated, inadvertently, as our errand boy. This is why, leading up to this doxology for today, Paul prays that we will be filled with the Holy Spirit – 'all the fullness of God'. The truth is that we don't know how to pray in accordance with how God would have us pray: 'We do not know what we ought to pray for, but the Spirit himself intercedes for us.' *Matthew 6:8*

Romans 8:26

A song by Rory Noland and Greg Ferguson says:

> He is able, more than able to do much more than I
> could ever dream.
> He is able, more than able to make me what he wants
> me to be.[20] *SASB 836*

Although God is able to do more than all we ask or imagine, whether he does depends on where we are with him. God could have opened the floodgates of Heaven and poured out more blessings than the nation could cope with, but he didn't because the people withheld what was rightfully his. So, are *we* fully surrendered to God? Are we filled with his Spirit? Are our requests focused on what he desires, fulfilling his will and purpose – his glory? *Malachi 3:7-12*

PRAYER
Fill me with your Spirit, Lord, that I may desire what you desire and bring you glory.

More than meets the eye

To him who is able to keep you from stumbling and to present you before his glorious presence without fault and with great joy ... be glory, majesty, power and authority (vv 24-25)

THERE are those who believe Mary was a virgin all her life and Jesus was her only child, when biblical evidence suggests otherwise. Matthew 1:25 states the marriage of Mary and Joseph was not consummated until after Jesus' birth, implying a normal marital relationship followed. Referring to Jesus as Mary's firstborn, Luke 2:7 suggests there were further children.

According to Mark 6:3 Jesus had four brothers, James, Joseph, Judas and Simon, and at least two sisters. John 2:12 speaks of Jesus' brothers accompanying him to Capernaum. Mark 3:20-21 and 31-35 say his brothers, thinking him mad, went with Mary to take charge of him, and in John 7:1-10 we are told that his brothers did not believe in him.

But, following Christ's ascension, Acts 1:14 records that his brothers and mother were with the disciples in prayer in the upper room. Galatians 1:19 refers to James, who was head of the Jerusalem church, being the Lord's brother, and 1 Corinthians 9:5 indicates some or all of Jesus' brothers married and became itinerant ministers of the gospel.

Was it the death and resurrection of Jesus that brought about the extraordinary change in his brothers? How could they have lived with him so long and yet been so blind? Yet some of us can testify to having been in close proximity to Jesus long before we woke up to the reality of who he was.

Most scholars agree that Jesus' brother, Judas or Jude, wrote this short book. Though not an easy book, Jude concludes with encouragement and assurance that God is able to keep us from stumbling and present us into his breathtakingly glorious presence without fault. Our sins have been attributed to Another.

We will appear sinless, unblemished. It will be an occasion of great joy, not one of fear and trembling, with all sin, shame and sorrow gone.

PRAYER
Lord, you may have gone to the Cross feeling you had failed as far as your brothers were concerned. Help us, when we feel we have failed, to take heart in the fact that things are not always as they appear to be.

Being a blessing to God

Bless the LORD, O my soul: and all that is within me, bless his holy name. Bless the LORD, O my soul, and forget not all his benefits (vv 1-2 *KJV*)

HOW can we bless God when he is the source of all blessings? When God blesses us we are the beneficiaries of the help, strength, gifts and various other things we need. God has no needs. We cannot give him anything he does not already have – other than our praise and thanksgiving.

Much in the Bible is about God blessing us and the benefits we receive from him. This psalm certainly is! We may have dark and difficult days, trying and tragic times, when Satan turns our attention away from all that God is and has done for us. The devil tempts us to question God's love and care whenever we experience something bewilderingly awful. What we are feeling can so easily undermine our faith.

But, 'Forget not all his benefits,' the psalmist cries before going on to list them. He reminds us that we have known God's forgiveness, his healing, him saving us from dangers, his love and compassion. God hasn't treated us as our sins deserved and, although life is short and we are soon gone, it isn't the end for we who fear God. His crowning blessing is the promise of eternal life – 'from everlasting to everlasting,' as verse 17 puts it.

So, how do we bless God in response to all of this? By being ever aware, focused on and grateful to God for such benevolence and a love that cost him everything. By praising and thanking him from our innermost being. Of course, our worship and praise is not confined to religious services and meetings. It's a 24/7 thing expressed in every facet of our lives. Our one aim and longing in life is that of pleasing God.

(see Romans 12:1-2)

In the film *Chariots of Fire*, the writer Colin Welland put these memorable words in the mouth of Eric Liddell: 'I believe God made me for a purpose. But he also made me fast, and when I run I feel his pleasure.'

PRAYER

Dear Father, make me a blessing to you. Fill me with your Holy Spirit so that pleasing you will be my one and only desire in all I think, say and do, that in me others might see Jesus.

Notes

Some of this information is taken from books in the personal possession of the writers. Therefore, the editions listed may not be the latest available and some may be out of print.

1   'The Missing Person' by Alan Redpath was extracted from *Christian Life* magazine and appeared in 'Reflections – Classic and Contemporary Excerpts' in *Christianity Today*, 13 December 1985

2   © 2004 worshiptogether.com songs, sixsteps Music (Admin. by kingswaysongs.com) Alletrop Music/Music Services (Admin. by Song Solutions www.songsolutions.org)

3   © 1993 Make Way Music www.grahamkendrick.co.uk

4   www.oxfordlearnersdictionaries.com

5   Joe Kapolyo, 'Matthew', in *Africa Bible Commentary* 2010, edited by Tokunboh Adeyemo, WordAlive Publishers, Nairobi, Kenya; and Zondervan, Grand Rapids, Michigan, USA, page 1144

6   Ibid 5

7   Dale Carnegie, *How to Stop Worrying and Start Living*, Diamond Pocket Books Pvt Ltd, New Delhi, India, 2016

8   www.biblegateway.com/resources/encyclopedia-of-the-bible/carmel

9   www.biblegateway.com/resources/encyclopedia-of-the-bible/sharon

10 *The Message of Acts* study guide, © 1991 Inter-Varsity Press, Nottingham, England

11 'Without You', published in *Sing to the Lord* (Mixed Voices) vol 13 part 2, © 2006 SP&S Ltd

12 © Hope Publishing Company, Carol Stream, IL 609188. All rights reserved. Used by permission

13 © 1990 Vineyard Songs Canada and Mercy Vineyard Publishing (Admin. by Song Solutions www.songsolutions.org)

14 Fred B. Craddock, *As One Without Authority*, Chalice Press, Tennessee, USA, 2001

15 Ron Buckland, *Children and the Gospel*, Scripture Union, Australia, 2002

16 Jean-Pierre de Caussade, *Abandonment to Divine Providence*, translated by John Beevers, Image Books, Doubleday Dell Publishing Group, New York, USA, 1975

17 Constance M. Cherry, *The Worship Architect*, Baker Academic, Michigan, USA, 2010

18 Fleming Rutledge, *The Undoing of Death*, William B. Eerdmans Publishing Co, Michigan, USA, 2002

19 'King of kings', words and music by Jason Ingram, Brooke Ligertwood and Scott Ligertwood, © 2019 Hillsong Music Publishing

20 © 1989 Maranatha! Praise Inc./Universal Music/Small Stone Media BV, Holland (Print/Sync UK/ Eire by Song Solutions www.songsolutions.org)

Index
January–April 2022 (as from January–April 2020)

2 Thessalonians
January–April 2020
May–August 2021
3 January–April 2022

1 Timothy
September–December 2021
6 May–August 2021

2 Timothy
September–December 2021

Titus
September–December 2021
3 May–August 2020

Philemon
September–December 2021

Hebrews
September–December 2020
1–5 May–August 2021
4 January–April 2020
4 September–December 2021
7–8 May–August 2021
8 January–April 2022
10 May–August 2020
10 September–December 2021
10–13 May–August 2021

James
September–December 2021
2 January–April 2020

1 Peter
1 January–April 2022
5 May–August 2021

2 Peter
3 September–December 2021

1 John
January–April 2021
September–December 2021
4 May–August 2021

2 John
January–April 2021
September–December 2021

3 John
January–April 2021
September–December 2021

Jude
May–August 2020
September–December 2021
January–April 2022

Revelation
1 January–April 2020
19 September–December 2020

Subscribe

Words of Life is published three times a year, in January-April, May
and September-December. *There are four easy ways to subscribe.*

1. Post: complete and return the subscription form below (please note เ.
details required for Gift Subscriptions).

2. Phone: +44 (0) 1933 445445.

3. Online: sar.my/wolsubu (UK), sar.my/wolsubeu (europe), sar.my/wolsubrow
(rest of the world) or sar.my/wolsubgift (gift subscriptions).

4. Visit: your local church or high street bookshop can order copies for you.

SUBSCRIPTION FORM

Name (Miss/Mrs/Ms/Mr)..

Address..

.... Postcode ....

Tel.No................................. Email*...................................

Annual Subscription Rates† including postage and packaging:
UK £15.95   **Europe** £20.95   **Rest of the world** £25.95

Please send me .... copy/copies of the next three issues of *Words of Life*
commencing with **May-August 2022.**

Total: £ .... **I enclose payment by cheque** ☐
Please make cheques payable to *The Salvation Army*

Please debit my Visa / Mastercard / Switch / Maestro card:

Card No. ☐☐☐☐ ☐☐☐☐ ☐☐☐☐ ☐☐☐☐

Security No. ☐☐☐ **Issue no (Maestro)** _____ **Expiry date:** _____ /_____

Cardholder's signature: .... **Date:** ....

GIFT SUBSCRIPTION FORM

Please provide details of the recipient of your Gift Subscription below. Ensure
you provide your full address and payment details in the main Subscription
section above, as these are required to process payments made by credit card.

Name (Miss/Mrs/Ms/Mr)..

Address..

.... Postcode........................

*Send this form and any cheques to: The Mail Order Department, Salvationist Publishing
and Supplies, 66-78 Denington Road, Denington Industrial Estate, Wellingborough,
Northamptonshire NN8 2QH, UK, or contact your local Salvation Army church for details
of your nearest territorial/command supplies department, which can order copies for you.*

☐ * We would like to keep in touch with you via our mailing list. If you prefer not to receive correspond-
ence from us, please tick this box. The Salvation Army does not sell or lease its mailing lists.

† *Subscription rates are subject to change without notice.*